COMPLETE
EVANGELISM

The Luke-Acts Model

Pedrito U. Maynard-Reid

HERALD PRESS
Scottdale, Pennsylvania
Waterloo, Ontario

Library of Congress Cataloging-in-Publication Data
Maynard-Reid, Pedrito U.
    Complete evangelism : the Luke-Acts model / Pedrito U.
Maynard-Reid.
        p. cm.
    Includes bibliographical references and index.
    ISBN 0-8361-9045-9 (alk. paper)
    1. Evangelistic work. 2. Missions—Theory. 3. Church work.
4. Church and social problems. 5. Bible. N.T. Luke—Criticism,
interpretation, etc. 6. Bible. N.T. Acts—Criticism.
interpretation, etc. I. Title.
BV3770.M39 1996
269'.2—dc20   96-33203

The paper used in this book is recycled and meets the minimum requirements of American National Standard for Information Sciences—
Permanence of Paper for Printed Library Materials, ANSI Z39.48-1984.

COMPLETE EVANGELISM
Copyright © 1997 by Herald Press, Scottdale, Pa. 15683
    Published simultaneously in Canada by Herald Press,
    Waterloo, Ont. N2L 6H7. All rights reserved
Library of Congress Catalog Number: 96-33203
International Standard Book Number: 0-8361-9045-9
Printed in the United States of America
Book design by Jim Butti

06 05 04 03 02 01 00 99 98 97 10 9 8 7 6 5 4 3 2 1

To my mother,
Edith Maynard-Reid,
whose concern for the whole person
has inspired me

The Spirit of the Lord is upon me,
  because he has anointed me
    to bring good news to the poor.
He has sent me
  to proclaim release to the captives
    and recovery of sight to the blind,
  to let the oppressed go free,
  to proclaim the year of the Lord's favor....
Today this scripture has been fulfilled in your hearing.

—Jesus, in Luke 4

They devoted themselves
  to the apostles' teaching
    and fellowship,
  to the breaking of bread
    and the prayers....
There was not a needy person among them.

—Luke, in Acts 2 and 4

Contents

Foreword by Charles Van Engen 7
Preface 10
Introduction 13

1. HISTORICAL OVERVIEW 17
   Pre-Civil War 18
   From Nineteenth to Twentieth Century 22
   The Fundamentalist-Modernist Debate 28
   World War II to 1960 33
   The 1960s 35
   The 1970s 36
   The 1980s 41
   The 1990s 44

2. HERMENEUTICAL METHOD 46
   Competing Models 48
   A Contextual Model 52

3. READING LUKE-ACTS AGAIN 59
   Defining Evangelism 59
   Trajectory Through Luke-Acts 64
   Hope 65
   Challenge 79

4. THEOLOGICAL MOTIFS IN LUKE-ACTS 92
  The Reign of God 93
  Salvation 98
  Repentance 109
  Conversion 116
  The Holy Spirit 120

5. MISSIOLOGICAL IMPLICATIONS 123
  Evangelism: The Debate 124
  The Lukan Paradigm 135
    Hope 138
    Challenge 142
  Contextual and Incarnational 150
    A Relevant Approach 150
    A Lived Approach 156

CONCLUSION 159

Notes 162
Bibliography 168
Index 177
The Author 183

Documentation

Notes in parentheses refer to items listed in the Bibliography. Information includes the author's last name (and first initial if necessary for identification), year of publication (if needed to distinguish the book in the Bibliography), volume number (if needed), and page number.

Foreword

Complete Evangelism! What a refreshing, realistic, and motivating approach to the most essential task for which the church exists! What should change when the gospel of Jesus Christ is proclaimed? Pedrito U. Maynard-Reid is right on target when he answers, *All of life, both personal and social.*

For the past seventy-five years, people involved in missions and evangelism have been plagued by a dichotomy that should never have happened. Early in this book, Maynard-Reid masterfully summarizes how, through the nineteenth century, missions and evangelism in North America sought to bring about the wholistic transformation of all of life. This included both personal and social dimensions, vertical in relation to God and horizontal in relation to other persons and society.

How sad that in the first three decades of the twentieth century, this "complete" view of evangelization was torn apart for a number of reasons documented here by Maynard-Reid. It is equally unfortunate that this false and unbiblical dichotomy between so-called "evangelism" and "social action" has been exported by Protestant missions to the rest of the world, causing strife and division among Christians and churches in Africa, Asia, Latin America, and Oceania.

Since World War II, evangelicals have struggled to find ways to bring these two poles together again. Maynard-

Reid introduces the reader to many of the most important thinkers, conferences, and documents that have come from this search. But he is right when he says, "The relation of personal salvation to social transformation is still not yet resolved. We are at the turn of another century, and the debate continues" (45). So the author sets out to "build [a new synthesis] upon a foundation which is rooted in Scripture, particularly in the life and ministry of Jesus Christ [as focused in Luke's perspective of evangelism]" (45).

Maynard-Reid has done what he proposed. Guided by a hermeneutical approach to Scripture that is itself wholistic and takes seriously the breadth of viewpoints found in the Bible, he helps us read Luke-Acts again. Maynard-Reid is a worthy guide in this new reading, for he listens intently to Luke and carefully balances his own understanding of the two sides of the issue, holding firmly to both personal and social aspects of salvation.

In this new reading we discover that Luke the missionary evangelist did not split evangelism into either-or categories. I believe Maynard-Reid's understanding of Luke is accurate: Luke did not divide personal from social dimensions. He has done the Christian church a wonderful service by helping us, through Luke's eyes, to see the world and God's salvation in our world.

This book's excellent organization, clear flow, and readable style helps all of us gain a new appreciation for the way Luke-Acts can contribute to erasing the artificial dichotomy that has plagued us for so long. Here we see Luke's perspectives on hope for the marginalized, challenge to the powerful, and theological themes on the reign of God, salvation, repentance, conversion, and the Holy Spirit. At every point in his reading of Luke-Acts, Pedrito helps the reader gain a vision for a *Complete Evangelism* that transforms all of life, both personal and social.

In this powerful, motivating, and insightful book, Maynard-Reid has offered us a vision of *Complete Evangelism* that challenges and informs all of us involved in the proclamation of the gospel in our various contexts, in this century and the next. Anyone interested in evangelism and mission will find here a helpful and accessible guide. I, for one, plan to use it as a text in my classes.

Head, heart, and hand combine in Maynard-Reid's reading of Luke, in the way he has written this book, and in his understanding of what mission and evangelism ought to look like. This new vision can become reality once we move beyond the unacceptable dichotomy that has created so much pain, conflict, and confusion in the church's mission during the twentieth century.

This is more than a book on evangelism, it is more than a commentary on Luke-Acts, and it is more than a discussion of an issue in missiological theory. It is all of these. However, it is also a passionate, sensitive, careful, and clear call to the church to offer our world today the gospel of Jesus Christ in all its transformational fullness. Let's join the author in discovering new ways for the church to live out in word and deed a *Complete Evangelism*.

Charles Van Engen
Arthur F. Glasser Professor of Biblical Theology of Mission
School of World Mission, Fuller Theological Seminary

Preface

This book arises out of a long-standing interest in relating three areas of religious life and study: evangelism; social action; and careful, critical biblical study. My mother, Edith Maynard-Reid, has been influential in nurturing and fostering all three areas since my childhood. I count her wisdom as invaluable in implicitly helping me to integrate these areas wholistically in my ministry. To her I dedicate this book.

Building on this foundation, I decided to make a scholarly and systematic integration of evangelism, social action, and biblical study. This task has developed in stages. It began with many graduate courses at Andrews University Theological Seminary in the 1970s. I'm especially indebted to professors who, in those formative years, exposed me to additional new and exciting ways to look at the Scriptures in depth, and to read each book contextually. Such teachers include James Cox, William Johnsson, Abraham Terian, Larry Geraty, Ivan Blazen, Sakae Kubo, and Leona Running.

The second stage of the integration process took place as I wrote my doctoral dissertation. I studied the epistle of James not only exegetically, using the traditional tools of biblical interpretation, but through preparing a description of the social world of the community of James. I concluded, as demonstrated in my book *Poverty and Wealth in the Epistle of James* (Orbis, 1987), that the biblical authors were not ivory-tower theologians interested only in individual spiritual concerns; instead, they were also social activists.

The third and final stage of my analysis on this subject began to take place as I pursued postgraduate work at Fuller Theological Seminary School of World Mission. Courses in church growth by C. Peter Wagner and Charles Van Engen were invaluable. I am in their debt. However, as I carefully studied the church-growth methods developed by Donald McGavran, I saw that he relegated social action to a minuscule place in the evangelistic enterprise; this seemed faulty and unbiblical.

I offer this book in an attempt to play a small role in repairing the stark dichotomy between evangelism and social action which is so foundational in the church-growth movement and in much of evangelical Christianity. I hope that the model presented here in the new reading of Luke-Acts demonstrates that the evangelistic task in the life and ministry of Jesus and the early church was wholistic—one in which personal and social evangelism worked hand in hand.

Without the aid of colleagues, friends, and family members, this book would not have come to fruition. I am grateful to Walla Walla College for granting me summers off from teaching in order to concentrate on grappling with the complex academic missiological discussions. Particularly my colleagues in the School of Theology must be singled out for their scholarly engagement as well as their lighthearted bantering; these all played significant roles in the formulation of positions presented in this work.

Enough praise cannot be heaped upon my friend and adopted family member Lorraine Jacobs, who not only typed the manuscript but also did major editorial work to enhance its quality and readability. Special thanks also go to my sister Dr. Audrey Reid and her family in California. They housed me, fed me, and put up with my eccentricities during many summers and sabbaticals as I worked on this book.

Without the support and encouragement of my dearest wife, Violet, and my children, Pedrito II and Natasha, this book would not be seeing the light of day. They have endured more than anyone should ask their family to endure. Fatherless and husbandless summers, days locked away in the study, and even when we were together the absentminded-professor syndrome signaling "present in the body, but absent in the spirit"—these were tolerated with grace, patience, and love. I am eternally in debt to my immediate family.

It is my sincerest desire that this book will enhance the reign of God in this world. I do not intend it to be divisively confrontational. I put it forth with the intent that the voice of the Scripture be heard afresh, and that the life and teachings of Jesus be recaptured completely and prophetically. I hope that when evangelism and social action are integrated wholistically, the church will be renewed and revitalized, and the reign of God will be more fully realized "today," as Jesus said in the synagogue at Nazareth.

Pedrito U. Maynard-Reid
Walla Walla College
College Place, Washington

Introduction

Since around 1900, there has been a growing dichotomy between evangelism and social action. In this posed contrast, evangelism is taken to be a spiritual and personal enterprise in which an individual is called to reject personal sins and accept Jesus as Lord, in preparation for Christ's second coming.

In this book I show that such a dichotomy is false and unbiblical. This supposed contradiction between evangelism and social action is rooted in a gnostic worldview with a dualistic conception of the universe and humankind. Such a worldview separates the private from the public, the internal from the external, the spiritual from the social. I argue that when one recaptures the biblical worldview, true evangelism is a whole. It involves both personal and social components; both are equally valid without one holding priority over the other.

The issue is whether evangelism should include a social component or not, or how to prioritize the two dimensions. This is one of the thorniest areas in missiological and theological studies today. The present dilemma arose out of the fundamentalist-modernist debate of the early decades of the twentieth century. My first chapter will survey the historical life situations that have entrapped us and left us with a dichotomized view of evangelism.

Those who hold to the gnostic view of evangelism seek their support by a selective reading of Scripture. Particularly, the great commission (Matt. 28:18-20) has become the paradigm for mission. Though the New Testament nowhere upholds these verses as the sole overriding mandate for evangelism, it is almost impossible to dethrone this passage from its dominant, solo reign. However, believers do need to recognize in other texts equally valid models for mission and evangelism. Yet if the great commission is truly followed, "teaching [disciples] to obey everything [Jesus has] commanded" (28:20) is quite a comprehensive assignment, as shown in Matthew 5–8, 10!

The second chapter will address this hermeneutical question, explaining how Scripture should be read as one tries to get a handle on defining evangelism. Is there a prescriptive, absolute, authoritative definition? Or is the definition descriptive and multidimensional? Does the New Testament contain a theoretical and rational definition, or does evangelism derive its definition contextually? Can the Scriptures still be authoritative even though authors, under the influence of the Holy Spirit, develop theology and missiology to fit their particular contexts?

In the next two chapters, as an illustration of my thesis, I give a hermeneutical overview of Luke-Acts through a fresh reading and by identifying its theological motifs. As we reread this two-volume document, I show that it does present a wholistic paradigm or model for evangelism. Luke will be highlighted as a theologian who uniquely edited and created his work to emphasize the powerful social dimension of the evangelist's task, without diminishing the personal and internal aspects.

The personal *and* the social are involved in Luke's perspective of the ministries of John the Baptist, Jesus, the primitive church, and Paul. Socioeconomic, political, and personal transformation of individual and corporate structures—this is at the heart of Luke's theology. My longitudinal and theological analysis of his work demonstrates that evangelism, seen as an invitation to the reign of God and an initiation into it, has both an earthly and heavenly focus, a present and future reality. Evangelism for Luke not only gives hope to the spiritually and socially oppressed but is confrontive as it challenges the spiritual and social powers which oppose the reign of God.

If biblical evangelism is wholistic, and if the context of Luke-Acts is to determine the practice of the evangelistic enterprise, then we must seek models of evangelism that are similarly wholistic and suited to unique contexts. This I seek to explore in the final chapter by analyzing and applying missiological implications from Luke Acts. I briefly propose some suggestions or principles on how evangelism should be uniquely transformational, both individually and corporately, personally and socially. I will do this with reference to my present setting as a Seventh-Day Ad ventist in the Northwest of the United States and to my previous situation in the Caribbean.

This study is primarily focused on evangelical concerns rather than on ecumenical, mainline Protestant, Roman Catholic, or Orthodox issues of evangelization. We certainly may learn from each other, and I will refer to the work of those in other Christian streams and extrapolate much of value. But my target audience is evangelicals who have a particularly strong traditional belief in the authority and inspiration of Scripture.

This is far from being an exhaustive study; it is not meant to be. I present it as another drop in the bucket for those of us who desire to reinvent evangelism and recapture the total, whole, transforming grace and love of our Lord and Savior Jesus Christ.

1

Historical Overview

A thorough and careful reading of Christian history reveals a startling fact: renewal movements engaging in missions and evangelistic outreach never failed to include the social transformation of the individual and society as part of their task. The biblical records portray the post-resurrection Christian community as a socially aware body. Secular writers also recognized this unusual dimension of their existence.

Aristides, a Roman, described the early Christians to the emperor Hadrian thus:

> They love one another. They never fail to help widows; they save orphans from those who would hurt them. If they have something, they give freely to the man who has nothing; if they see a stranger, they take him home, and are happy, as though he were a real brother. They don't consider themselves brothers in the usual sense, but brothers instead through the Spirit in God. (from Miles: 125. *See* Bibliography)

Mission historians are becoming more aware that this dimension of Christianity never ceased. It is now being recognized that virtually all missionary movements throughout Christian history have been concerned about social outreaches and community development and involved in them. This dimension was never separate from the task of communicating the gospel but was regularly part of it.

There is a remarkable degree of consistency in history: Christian missionary outreaches have been focusing on education, health care, agriculture, and other kinds of social uplift programs for the marginal and neglected members of society (Pierson: 18). Such an understanding of the missionary evangelistic task continued into the Great Awakenings of the eighteenth and nineteenth centuries.[1]

Pre-Civil War

Evangelical Christians were at the forefront of social reform worldwide in the early nineteenth century. For example, the Clapham Sect, a group of evangelical aristocratic politicians, bankers, and Anglican clergy of Clapham and Cambridge (England) gathered at the home of William Wilberforce and strategized reform. The focus was on both personal salvation and moral and social reforms.

Wilberforce and Anthony Ashley Cooper, the seventh Lord Shaftesbury, stand out as the most famous members. Wilberforce is widely known as the major force behind the abolition of slavery. Shaftesbury was just as powerful in his attack on the chimney-sweeps scandal, child labor in factories, female labor in the mines, extra-long working hours, the lack of safety and medical protection, and many unhealthy working conditions (Miles: 47-49). Attacking these was part of their evangelical Christian responsibility.

In the early days of the Protestant missionary movement, missionary societies like the renewal movements before them were also involved in this type of social initiative. Yet within the societies, debates began to develop on whether social action was a proper part of the missionary task. Some justified it, calling it preparation for the gospel. Thus schools, hospitals, and other social institutions were established (Costas: 65). For many in those early days, it was unthinkable to separate the proclamation of the good news of salvation from the social dimensions of life.

During the second Great Awakening (1790s-1850s), almost every Protestant denomination was engaged in social services. High on their agenda were issues such as women's rights, temperance, prison reform, public education, world peace, and the abolition of slavery (Ro: 29).

William Pannell (7), summarizing the church's social action in the nineteenth century, states that as early as 1845, churches were involved in urban ministry to the poor. For example, both Baptists and Methodists offered skilled education for the poor. They demonstrated that Christian responsibility to human beings goes beyond saving their souls.

This was the position of a number of prominent evangelists. Chief among them was Charles Finney, one of the most famous American evangelists during the second Awakening, and president of Oberlin College in 1851-66. Delos Miles (49) suggests that Finney may have been the foremost promoter of revivals and social reform during the nineteenth century. Finney proclaimed that revivals are hindered when churches and ministers take the wrong stand on human rights. He argued that reforming the world must be a commitment of the Christian reformer.

Miles notes that "long before the advent of liberation theology, Finney recognized that God had a preference for the poor" (50). Finney's evangelism led individuals to take a personal stand for Christ as Lord in their lives; it also led to the establishment of such social institutions as elementary and secondary schools and colleges (Ro: 29).

The Millerites were a movement with which Charles Finney associated in the early 1840s. This evangelistic renewal movement, from which the Seventh-Day Adventist Church evolved, also had a wholistic view of spirituality. They insisted that a social dimension must be recognized as an important component of the spiritual dynamic. Religious enthusiasm for the impending second advent of Christ (which they predicted would be in 1843; then after that disappointment, 1844) and social concern went hand in hand, as was common in many reform movements in the nineteenth century.

Ingemar Linden suggests that "the fact that Millerism welcomed all manner of ideas on social reform, can be explained partly because it lacked the conservatism of an established organization" (57). Perhaps the Millerites were simply being biblical in their wholistic theology, or were caught up in the religious and social renewal of the pre-Civil War Awakening. Whatever the explanation, the fact remains that Millerism penetrated into districts where the evils of urbanization and industrialization flourished.

Chief among the social Millerite reformers was Joshua V. Himes, its leading organizer. He was involved in the emancipation of African-American slaves, temperance, women's rights, pacifism, and rapproachment between denominations. He was correctly dubbed "a radical of the radicals." So also was the Presbyterian pastor Charles Fitch, a social activist. After writing *Slaveholding Weighed in the Balance of Truth* in 1837, he formed the Evangelical Abolitionist Society (Strayer: 9).

Thus in this early period, evangelicals and renewal movements were convinced that personal sins had communal roots and had to be addressed in their totality. Personal salvation and personal sin were never solitary. The presentation of the good news of Jesus Christ and preparation for his coming included a powerful social component.

Timothy Smith, however, expresses the opinion that most evangelists prior to 1865 were preoccupied with personal religious experience. Their chief concern was preparing persons for another world. Opposition to social evils, he suggests, was for the most part "only an occasional skirmish in the war on personal wickedness."

For example, Charles Finney inspired many abolitionists but he never thought of himself as an abolitionist (T. Smith: 149). "Liberalism on social issues, not reactions, was the dominant note which evangelical preachers sounded before 1860" (151). Yet Smith shows that many influential evangelists "defined carefully the relationship between personal salvation and community improvement and never tired of giving glowing descriptions of the social and economic millennium which they believed revival Christianity would bring into existence" (151).

The quest for personal perfection in these years prior to the Civil War was also at the heart of evangelical social concern. It is Smith's thesis that this quest, "joined with compassion for poor and needy sinners and a rebirth of millennial expectation," made popular Protestantism a powerful social force long before the conflict over slavery erupted into war (T. Smith: 149).

Not only were some Methodist perfectionists seeking to overthrow slavery, intemperance, political corruption, and other public vices. They were also decrying the increase of personal wealth, stating that it was the most subtle enemy of a life of personal consecration. True dedication, they argued, was one of service to others. This is what the gospel demands (T. Smith: 155).

This call for a more and purer piety to achieve the successful destruction of social and political evils spread throughout the churches after 1835. The social potency of this doctrine reached a white heat in the Oberlin and Wesleyan experience of sanctification. This included "ethical seriousness, the call to full personal consecration, the belief in God's immanence, in his readiness to transform the present world through the outpoured Holy Ghost, and the exaltation of Christian love" (T. Smith: 154).

The social implications of this filtered into the Methodist belief in deliverance from all sin and entire consecration (T. Smith: 160-161). William Arthur, a Methodist perfectionist, said in his 1880 book *The Tongue of Fire*, "Nothing short of the general renewal of society ought to satisfy any soldier of Christ" (from T. Smith: 154). This sanctification-perfectionist theology and experience placed Methodists and other similar Protestant evangelicals in a position to be socially conscious.

The revivals and evangelical Awakenings of the first half of the nineteenth century were rooted in a composite of theology and experience that was wholistic—personal and social. In 1858-59 a revival of Pentecostal proportions occurred; its roots were in previous decades. The revival convinced people that the destruction of social and political evils was imminent. These evils would be destroyed by the force of the gospel (T. Smith: 153).

This revival just before the Civil War differed from previous revivals in the scope of involvement. Many persons who were not class leaders, exhorters, and social preachers got caught up in the euphoria of social and personal transformation. Lay businesspersons organized daily prayer meetings and used Christian principles to enhance social changes. Among these laypersons was D. L. Moody. Typical of the lay concern for society's welfare was Moody's support of the YMCA (Ro: 29-30).

From Nineteenth to Twentieth Century

The debate over the extent to which Christians should be involved in social action, begun in the first half of the

nineteenth century, gained momentum after the Civil War
and reached its zenith around World War II. Yet for the
most part, pre-World War I evangelicals and mission pro-
moters saw no dichotomy between evangelism and social
involvement.

Famous nineteenth-century evangelicals argued, for
example, that urban evangelism and social responsibility
could not be separated. These included A. B. Simpson of
the Christian Missionary Alliance, Florence and Charles
Crittondon, J. A. McAuley, and Kate and Waller Barrett.
Many of these, says William Pannell, came out of the Wesleyan tradition and were called to social action by the
squalor and misery in the city. "They knew that holiness of
life could not allow suffering and injustice to prevail when
it was within the power of God's people to do something
about it" (Pannell: 8-9; see also Patterson: 76).

During this period there was in general a rapid growth
of evangelical concern with social issues. Matters such as
poverty, the rights of the working class, the liquor traffic,
slum housing, and racial bitterness took center stage in the
program of many evangelical Christians—to a larger degree than prior to the Civil War. Many went far beyond the
earlier emphasis on almsgiving and handouts. There was a
widespread search to find the causes of human suffering,
and a concerted campaign to reconstruct social and economic relations after a Christian pattern (T. Smith: 148).

The social-gospel phenomenon at the turn of the
twentieth century was not the sole prerogative of liberal
Christianity. Many evangelicals, frustrated with the earlier
preoccupation on salvation from personal sin and a life
hereafter, changed to have a predominant social concern.
Thus the social-gospel movement arose as a reaction by a
cross-section of Christianity to a vertical religion at the expense of the horizontal.[2]

The social gospel found fertile soil in which to flourish

a century ago. People were faced with increased industrialization in Europe and America, increased immigration from eastern and southern Europe to America, problems from urbanization, recurrent depressions, social tensions, and a myriad of other problems. These aroused the conscience of many Christians.

Accordingly, there was a shift of emphasis in evangelism from a vertical, individual, future eschatological understanding of the reign of God. The new stress was on a horizontal, communal, imminent conception of God's reign for the here and now, with God achieving that reign through the efforts of human beings (Ro: 31). It was becoming a consensus that the eschatological rule of God involved the social and moral transformation of society.

Note well that this consensus was not the perspective of only liberal Christianity. Even among Protestant missionary evangelical leaders, there was widespread support for defending a social dimension of mission as God worked through Christians.[3] For evangelical missionaries as well, it was not a matter of either individual evangelism or social evangelism; it was a both-and stance. The nineteenth-century Presbyterian mission scholar James Dennis illustrates this perspective.

Dennis argued that missions is a "sociological force" with an aim of elevating humanity. Prior to the fundamentalist-modernist debate, this is typical of evangelicals who supported a strong component in missions. Dennis laid out his thesis clearly in 1896 in "The Student's Lectures on Mission at Princeton Theological Seminary," which formed the basis of his three-volume seminal work.

Christianity has always been a religious force in the world. That is obvious, according to Dennis. It has been known as a religion of the heart—a maker of new persons with "purified and ennobled character, and they give birth to new ecclesiastical institutions" (1:23).

He asked, however, Does its mission also "advocate and seek to establish a more refined moral code for the domestic, social, commercial, philanthropic, and even national life of mankind?" (1:23). His answer was yes. Christian mission should not be seen as an exclusive religious crusade with merely an evangelistic aim. It has a more extensive scope and a wider comprehensive meaning. Mission has to be a factor in the social regeneration of the world—a sociological force "elevating human society, modifying traditional evils, and introducing reformatory ideals" (1:23).

On the question of priority, Dennis supported the position that the personal evangelistic aim is first, and ever will be first in its import and dignity. But social actions are nonetheless very important. He admits that the results of social actions are slower than evangelism and more indirect. The results come with more difficulty and are less pronounced than the fruit of the evangelistic endeavors.

The social dimension of mission has to contend with hereditary, physical, intellectual, and moral forces. It will "rudely disturb the hitherto undisputed supremacy of the individual, domestic, social, and national environment." It will "cross the path of many prevailing customs, and even in some cases, of religious conviction and practice" (Dennis, 1:24). It will challenge public sentiment, lapsed standards, and evil customs. "The social conflicts of Christian missions must therefore be fought at an enormous disadvantage against overwhelming odds, while their victories in this sphere must come gradually and with little visible éclat" (1:24).

There are some limitations in the social component of mission, however. Dennis, for example, argued that it should not include dealing with modern economic problems. He, however, was quick to add that this is so because the capitalistic issues of the West have not impinged on the life of the mission field. It is not the function of Western civilization to impose its economic worldview upon non-Western societies, Dennis claimed (1:25). This is not the aim of the sociological force of mission.

Without belaboring Dennis's program for mission, it might be helpful to outline his basic theoretical justification for the sociological scope of mission. First, he argued from solidarity: the social collapse, the effect of the Fall, has affected all, not just individuals. Thus there needs to be solidarity in reconstruction (1:52-53).

Second, Dennis argued from analogy based on the expansive power of material forces: the great natural material forces work with expansive power to produce positive results (such as electricity). We should expect the same of spiritual forces in the realm of special social activities (1:53-54).

Third, Dennis argued from analogy based upon the larger scope of moral evil: evil impacts social life, shapes social destiny, and affects the economic and ethical environment of human beings. Christian missions must reverse these trends (1:54).

Dennis also had some arguments based on religious history. First, the Old Testament legislation has a strong sociological spirit. No one can read the Mosaic code without coming to this conclusion (1:54-55). Second, there is the historic achievement of Christianity: the rise and fall of faith within Christendom, according to Dennis, is directly related to its national social life. In addition, many social reforms in the wider realm of history have their roots in Christianity (1:55-56).

What James Dennis outlined in this groundbreaking work makes it clear that at the turn of the century, there was a strong social movement within evangelical Christianity. It recognized that the purpose of the Christian missionary, evangelist, and layperson must include not only a personal ethic but a social one as well.

We must admit, however, that toward the end of the nineteenth century and the beginning of the twentieth, there began a decline in evangelical social concern and involvement. Many reasons for this have been proposed. Ro suggests that one of them is millennialism.

During the first half of the nineteenth century, premillennialists, postmillennialists, and amillennialists all worked together for spiritual, cultural, and social progress.[4] However, during the second half of that century, Edwardsean postmillennialists became "secularized and substituted human effort for the work of the Holy Spirit" (Ro: 30).

Because of this, many evangelicals lost interest in social reform, mistakenly thinking they had to give it up in favor of reliance on God's power. They objected to the loss of transcendence in many social betterment projects and withdrew their support for social reform.

Other components in the theological upheaval prior to World War I did not help the situation. Christians had to contend with Kantian philosophy, Darwinian evolution, the growing interest in and use of sociology and psychology, new understandings in the scientific world, new methodologies in biblical interpretation which attempted to take a closer look at the literary and historical contexts, and so on.

These all seemed to threaten the basic evangelical fundamental belief about the nature of reality, the nature of the human person, the role of God in creation, the nature of the Bible, and ultimately the historicity of Jesus and his special salvific work (L. Smith: 25). Such upheaval set the stage for possibly the greatest religious crisis of the twentieth century.

The Fundamentalist-Modernist Debate

The fundamentalist-modernist conflict during the 1920s and 1930s brought about a traumatic ecclesiastical schism that realigned American Protestantism. It shaped attitudes toward social concern and evangelism up to the present (Linder: 214; Patterson: 73). Robert Linder calls the period between 1918 and 1929 "the Blunting of the Evangelical Social Conscience" (211-220). After the controversies of this period, the terms *modernist* and *social gospel* became synonymous in the minds of most fundamentalists, who associated them with liberalism.

This was a period of retreat and separation. It came to be referred to as the "Great Reversal." All progressive social and political concern, whether personal, private, or public, was virtually eliminated among conservative evangelicals. Conservatives reversed their attitudes toward social involvement. George Marsden writes that "until that time American evangelicals had generally followed (for better or worse) major social and political trends, usually providing Christian versions of the prevailing views. Among liberal Protestants this pattern continued, . . . but among fundamentalists it was sharply arrested" (152).

Conservatives, as they reacted against proponents of the social gospel and their emphasis on an imminent eschatology, turned more to preaching a gospel which placed emphasis on saving individual souls for the world hereafter. They totally rejected the optimistic, postmillennianiꞔᵗ teaching which was popular in the nineteenth century. Instead, they embraced a dispensational-premillennialism, an antinaturalistic and antiprogressive scheme of history based on the literal fulfillment of Bible prophecies in this dispensation.

Dispensationalists like Cyrus Scofield (who in 1909 produced the *Scofield Reference Bible* with dispensationalist footnotes) promoted millennial teachings. According to them, the Scriptures prophesied that within the present dispensation, Christendom would apostatize and there would be a secret rapture of the saints, followed by the public Parousia (coming) of Christ seven years later. All social and political benefits for Christians would be postponed until the Parousia. Then all the saints would be with Christ during his reign of a thousand years in Jerusalem.

This otherworldliness of conservative evangelicals made it natural for them to refuse to come to terms with the scientific world, particularly in the realm of biology and anthropology. In turn, there was a major confrontation between those who accepted the possibility of evolution and those who rejected any such possibility.

The debate over evolution came to a head in 1925 with the Scopes "Monkey Trial," challenging a Tennessee law against teaching evolution in a public school. Fundamentalists won the court case; but it is the widely held opinion that they lost the hearts and minds of America. They dropped in public credibility and were equated with backward rural ignorance (I. Smith: 25; Linder: 214-216)

The fundamentalist-modernist controversy spilled over into the missionary enterprises. In a perceptive article, James Patterson spells out the scenario (73-91). Protestant concerns which existed in the missionary movement at the turn of the nineteenth century began to unravel in the 1920s and 1930s. Part of the blame can be placed at the feet of financial and cultural issues that plagued the mission agencies and all of Protestantism during this period. But the major devastation came from the fundamentalist-modernist debate.

On the right, church leaders held that fundamental theological verities were being compromised. But on the left, there was a clamor for a radically different approach to mission. Conservative fundamentalists emphasized the priority of personal evangelism and salvation, the centrali-

ty of Christ's divine nature, and his personal unique salvific work. These they used as measuring rods for their
missionaries and mission board officers, while challenging
social involvement and the growing ecumenism. By this
approach they hoped to stem the tide of liberalism.

The situation in the Presbyterian and Baptist denominations is of interest. In their Auburn Affirmation of 1924,
Presbyterians were calling for theological toleration. But
this agitated the Presbyterian right. The latter used the
document to hunt down modernists, liberals, and social
gospelers. The conservatives were convinced that these
modernists had infiltrated the mission boards and under-
mined their evangelical character. A parallel scenario was
happening among the Baptists.

Official responses of both Presbyterians and Baptists to
their conservative critics proved futile during the 1920s.
The fundamentalists, for example, rejected any framework
which included social action and ecumenism. In late 1923
the board of managers of the American Baptist Foreign
Missionary Society (ABFMS) drafted a statement in which
they made it clear that evangelism had a higher priority
than social witness:

> We definitely and positively repudiate the idea that
> social service is the supreme thing, and so far as we
> are aware, no one connected with our Society would
> think of substituting it for salvation. At the same time,
> we believe that we are following in the steps of our
> Master when we establish hospitals for the sick, and
> support other efforts to relieve human poverty and
> suffering. . . . Far from substituting social services for
> salvation, we teach that salvation of the individual and
> the world must be found in Christ, and we point men
> to him and his cross as the moving power for every
> form of service. (from Patterson: 81-82)

This statement was presented to the annual meeting in 1924 and adopted as a policy statement. It represented a delicate balancing act which affirmed the priority of personal evangelism. Yet at the same time, it refused to surrender the legitimacy of social action overseas. This was meant to appease the conservative fundamentalists, but it failed.

By the mid-1920s, fundamentalists had made an absolute and rigid dichotomy between evangelism and social action. In their circles, this nearly eliminated all progressive social and political involvement, both private and public. They, however, failed in their quest to exclude modernists from their denominations. But that was not their only failure. They failed to suppress the teaching of biological evolution in public schools; as noted earlier, they had lost the hearts of the majority of the American people. Their losses on all fronts left them in disarray as a social force, says Marsden (147).

Fundamentalists, however, regrouped and changed their character during the period of 1926-1940. From being a part of the mainstream American Protestantism, they moved in the direction of sectarianism. In many instances they formed or worked through independent churches and denominations, Bible institutes, and parachurch organizations. Through these avenues, fundamentalists returned to battle against modernists.

One of the most salient debates of this period grew out of the publication in 1932 of *Re-Thinking Missions*. As James Patterson discusses the dispute, he shows that the work was the culmination of a two-year project carried out by the Laymen's Foreign Missions Inquiry. It was financed and initiated by John D. Rockefeller Jr., a major donor to Baptist Missionary endeavors. His Institute of Social and Religious Research conducted the first phase of the study for the Laymen's Inquiry and presented the report.

Re-Thinking Missions suggested that the aim of missions was "to seek with people of other lands a true knowledge and love of God, expressing in life and word what we have learned through Jesus Christ, and endeavoring to give effect to his spirit in the life and the world" (from Patterson: 88).[5] The report emphasized evangelism through "living human service," with the hope that through quiet personal contact as well as by contagion the Christian way of life would be spread.

The report even went so far as to call for a separation of some social outreach from the proclamation task of evangelism:

> We believe, then, that the time has come to set the educational and other philanthropic aspect of mission work free from organizational responsibility to the work of conscious and direct evangelization. We must be willing to give largely without any preaching. (from Patterson: 88)

The report tended to give priority to social involvement.

Responses to *Re-Thinking Missions* spanned the theological spectrum. For example, the American Board of Commissioners for Foreign Missions (ABCFM of the Congregational churches) acknowledged that the spirit of the report is in line with the denomination's own thinking. Yet the ABCFM would love to see more emphasis given to the uniqueness of God's revelation in Christ.

A classic negative response came from the *Sunday School Times* in a January 7, 1933, article on "The Betrayal Commission: Report on the Layman's Foreign Missions Inquiry." It labeled the report "a strange, sinister, Satanic document" (from Patterson: 89). This appraisal expressed the sentiments and feelings of many fundamentalists.

Most Protestant mission leaders and boards responded to *Re-Thinking Missions* more in keeping with the earlier missionary consensus around 1900. They agreed that there was value in many of the report's practical suggestions. Yet at the same time, they were not willing to surrender traditional evangelical conceptions of missions.

By the time the debate had settled down, liberals, modernists, fundamentalists, and supporters of the consensus were deeply divided. Positions were polarized as to the nature and aim of mission. The fight over this work was the fatal blow to the missionary consensus. Even more important for us, the enduring legacy of this religious war is found even today in the polarized debate over evangelism versus social action.

World War II to 1960

In the 1940s and 1950s, evangelical theology was still in reaction to previous decades. Charles Van Engen calls it "over-against theology" (206). Because of the war, widespread pessimism intensified regarding humanity, culture, and the condition of the world. Evangelical conservatives felt that the old social-gospel mentality was empty. So they took a firm stand against any theology which smacked of "social gospelism." A classic work which took this reactionary and separatist fundamentalist viewpoint was Harold Lindsell's *A Christian Philosophy of Mission*.

Other evangelicals, however, began to take a second look at the subculture in which they lived. They began to object to the rigid mind-set of fundamentalism which ignored both science and culture. At the same time, they adhered to what they perceived as the basic fundamentals of Christian beliefs.

One of the most significant early critiques of the fundamentalists' retreat from social concern, representative of this latter viewpoint, was Carl Henry's *The Uneasy Con-*

science of Modern Fundamentalism. Published in 1947, it exploded like a bombshell (Linder: 221). This work was "an embryonic representative of the revisionary and mutualist 'neo-evangelical' position" (Van Engen, 1990:206). In it Henry expressed his concern for a new reformation in evangelical social attitudes. This work propelled him into the editor's chair of the magazine *Christianity Today.* From this pulpit he continued to prod evangelical Christians on social issues.

Carl Henry was joined later by a number of evangelicals who were also critical of the abdication of Christian social responsibility. These avoided the label "fundamentalists" because of the stigma associated with it. Instead, they chose to be called "neo-evangelicals," seeking to connect with pre-1900 evangelicalism while accepting modernity. This was later shortened to simply "evangelicals" (L. Smith: 27).

In the 1950s both fundamentalists and evangelicals became involved in social projects in the two-thirds world rather than at home. Educational, medical, agricultural, and other social ventures came into vogue. Yet while these mission agencies found themselves socioeconomically and politically active overseas, they spurned such activities at home in North America (Van Engen, 1990:211).

This period saw the overriding motivation for missions as the great commission of Matthew 28:18-20 and the proclamation of Christ's imminent return to usher in the millennium. Premillennialists, who comprised just about all conservative evangelicals, believed that once the gospel was preached to the whole world, the millennium would come. Their goal, therefore, was to give the gospel to every person, meaning every individual soul. "The social, political, economic, or cultural aspects of the lives of the unsaved were relatively unimportant compared to the question of heaven and hell" (Van Engen, 1990:210).

The 1960s

The social and political upheavals of the 1960s profoundly impacted the religious community. Linda Smith has accurately demonstrated that the widespread discontent in North America affected also the evangelical community. In particular, many young evangelicals began to be disillusioned by the apathy or even outright opposition of fundamentalists and evangelicals to the civil rights movement.

This younger generation started to question the lack of evangelical involvement in justice causes and commitment to them. Their questioning led them to ask "whether theological conservatism necessarily had to be tied to sociopolitical conservatism, especially if the latter reinforced a status quo of racism or exploitation" (L. Smith: 27). In subsequent decades, this inquiry led to a pivotal shift in direction by a significant number of the "children of the 60s." They began to recapture in new ways the evangelical worldview of the turn of the century, taking seriously the Christian's place in the world. Hence, they brought believers' perspectives to politics and to social issues which consumed society.

This rediscovery of the social dimensions of the gospel and how it can be made relevant also found its way onto the agendas of missionary conferences. At the Berlin World Congress on Evangelism in 1966, a number of these areas were explored. After that event, national and regional congresses jumped on the bandwagon and joined in the recovery and articulation of Christian social concern. Samuel Escobar says that it happened with "a surprising coincidence in contexts and tone" (306).

As would be expected, many of the papers presented at these forums had reference to what evangelicals had done in the past, such as the work of Wilberforce on the abolition of slavery, and other evangelical social reformers in Europe and North America. These examples reinforced their argument that evangelical social involvement was not simply a phenomenon with roots in the "wild sixties." Instead, it had grounding in evangelical history.

With this reorientation taking place, there necessarily had to be a shift in doing mission from the strongly individualistic perspective of recent decades, to an increased emphasis on community. Evangelism began again to be defined not only as proclamation for conversion; now it also involved social categories. As around 1900, missiologists engaged such disciplines as sociology, anthropology, and psychology to better grapple with this renewed perspective.

The 1970s

What stands out foremost in this decade is the fact that significant evangelical conferences began paying careful attention to social concerns. In 1973 fifty important evangelical leaders met together for a conference on Christian Faith and Politics. Among the attendees were older evangelicals like Carl Henry, Foy Valentine, Bernard Ramm, Frank Gaebelein, and Paul Rees. Younger ones included Ronald Sider, Jim Wallis, Paul Henry, Sharon Gallagher, and Samuel Escobar.

This group produced the Chicago Declaration of Evangelical Social Concern. According to Sider, it was one of the first major steps to recapture the social concern of evangelicals since the rupture early in this century (19). The declaration was far-reaching in its denunciation of racism, sexism, militarism, and materialism. It went further by giving a ringing call to repentance:

> We acknowledge that God requires justice. But we
> have not proclaimed or demonstrated his justice to an

unjust American society. Although the Lord calls us to defend the social and economic rights of the poor and the oppressed, we have mostly remained silent. We deplore the historic involvement of the church in America with racism and the conspicuous responsibility of the evangelical community for perpetuating the personal attitudes and institutional structures that have divided the body of Christ along color lines.

We call our fellow evangelical Christians to demonstrate repentance in a Christian discipleship that confronts the social and political injustice of our nation. (from Sider: 19)

The first major gathering to directly address the issue of evangelism and social concern, however, was the 1974 International Congress on World Evangelism held in Lausanne, Switzerland. Here we find evangelicals beginning to pull together social concern with personal evangelism. The covenant which resulted from the congress set up priorities between the two categories. Yet it was a major breakthrough in its comprehensiveness: personal, social, global, and cosmic. Paragraphs four and five are of significance for this study:

4. The Nature of Evangelism

To evangelize is to spread the good news that Jesus Christ died for our sins and was raised from the dead according to the Scriptures, and that as the reigning Lord he now offers the forgiveness of sins and the liberating gift of the Spirit to all who repent and believe. Our Christian presence in the world is indispensable to evangelism, and so is that kind of dialogue whose purpose is to listen sensitively in order to understand. But evangelism itself is the proclamation of the historical, biblical Christ as Savior and Lord, with a view to persuading people to come to him personally and so be reconciled to God. In issuing the gospel invitation we have no liberty to conceal the cost of discipleship. Jesus still calls all who would follow him to deny themselves, take up their cross, and identify themselves with his new community. The results of evangelism include obedience to Christ, incorporation into his church, and responsible service in the world (1 Cor. 15:3, 4; Acts 2:32-39; John 20:21; 1 Cor. 1:23; 2 Cor. 4, 5; 5:11, 20; Luke 14:25-33; Mark 8:34; Acts 2:40, 47; Mark 10:43-45).

5. Christian Social Responsibility

We affirm that God is both the Creator and the Judge of all men. We therefore should share his concern for justice and reconciliation throughout human society and for the liberation of men from every kind of oppression. Because mankind is made in the image of God, every person, regardless of race, religion, color, culture, class, sex, or age, has an intrinsic dignity because of which he should be respected and served, not exploited. Here too we express penitence both for our neglect and for having sometimes regarded evangelism and social concern as mutually exclusive. (Although reconciliation with man is not reconciliation with God, nor is social action evangelism, nor is political liberation salvation, nevertheless we affirm that evangelism and sociopolitical involvement are both part of our Christian duty. For both are necessary expressions of our doctrines of God and man, our love for our neighbor, and our obedience to Jesus Christ.) The message of salvation implies also a message of judgment upon every form of alienation, oppression, and discrimination, and we should not be afraid to denounce evil and injustice wherever they exist. When people receive Christ they are born again into his kingdom and must seek not only to exhibit but also to spread its righteousness in the midst of an unrighteous world. The salvation we claim should be transforming us in the totality of our personal and social responsibilities. Faith without works is dead. (Acts 17:26, 31; Gen. 18:25; Isa. 1:17; Ps. 45:7; Gen. 1:26, 27; James 3:9; Lev. 19:18; Luke 6:27, 35; James 2:14-26; John 3:3, 5; Matt. 5:20; 6:33; 2 Cor. 3:18; James 2:20).   (from Krass 1982:191-192)

This covenant demonstrated that within the family of evangelicals, there was a growing demand for a commitment to historical change and participation in the human struggle for justice, without lessening the importance of personal evangelism.

Although the document advocates a link between evangelism and social transformation, Titi Tienou is correct in noting that it does not clarify the nature of the link or their relationship (265). A sizable number of delegates signed a complementary and more radical statement that does not contradict the covenant but highlights the need for social involvement by Christians and emphasizes the dimensions of social justice (Castro: 29).

By the end of the 1970s, the momentum for social involvement had increased within evangelicalism. During this decade, there were more and more calls, even outside of conferences, for evangelicals to be more socially conscious and involved. The young evangelicals of the sixties who were involved in the civil rights and antiwar movements began to move into leadership positions in the seventies, as Linda Smith observes. So their causes were growing more visible, and so were black evangelicalism, feminine evangelicalism, and other concerns regarding lifestyle, hunger, and militarism (L. Smith: 29).

In 1973 Richard Mouw in *Political Evangelism* argued that political activity is an important aspect of the overall task of evangelism. But it was Jim Wallis, the founder and editor of the magazine *Sojourners*, who in 1976 made the most impact with *Agenda for a Biblical People*. In it he argued that "political and social realities must be comprehended and interpreted biblically, and the political character of the biblical witness must be rediscovered" (1976:4).

This movement, with Wallis as a leading figure, was critical of the conservative religious establishment for its lack of social consciousness. But it was just as critical of the religious left for its "lack of biblical rootage, its disregard for evangelism, and its lack of spiritual life and resources" (Wallis, 1976:10). It hoped for a proclamation and demonstration of a more wholistic gospel: one which would address all that places people in bondage, and all that oppresses people spiritually, economically, personally, and politically. The movement wanted a gospel which could "spark renewal and reconciliation among both religious conservatives and religious liberals" (10).

More evangelicals stood with the Lausanne Covenant and focused more on the primacy of personal salvation in the evangelistic enterprise. It was a period of evolution for many. John Stott, for example, stated that he no longer held the position that mission solely consisted of preaching, converting, and teaching; instead, it must be both social and evangelistic (Van Engen, 1990:220).

The church-growth movement, though supporting the Lausanne statement, continued to stress that many human agencies can relieve social needs, but only Christians have a message for soul salvation. The bottom line was that "eternal salvation is more important than temporal well-being" (McGavran: 23). Yet, because of the movement's strategy and philosophy of pragmatism, social involvement did play a role in the overall program of the church-growth movement (Van Engen, 1990:220).

The 1980s

As in the 1970s, evangelicals in the 1980s used major congresses, conferences, and consultations to highlight the relationship between personal evangelism and social concern and involvement. A 1980 world consultation organized by the Lausanne Committee for World Evangelization met in Pattaya, Thailand, to study in great depth questions of technique and methodologies in reaching specific groups.

However, a number of participants, particularly from the two-thirds world, requested that the discussion include the issue of justice and the responsibility of Christians to do justice. They noted that the Lausanne Covenant recognized the importance of justice in relation to evangelism, but the committee tended to focus heavily on the evangelistic dimension to the exclusion of the whole human situation. They requested that a world conference be convened to deal with the issue of social responsibility in relation to evangelism (Castro: 30-32).

In response to their concerns, two complementary meetings were called. The first was jointly organized by the Lausanne Committee for World Evangelization and the World Evangelical Fellowship. That 1982 Grand Rapids consultation specifically considered the relationship between evangelism and social responsibility.

The second was organized by the World Evangelical Fellowship in 1983 in Wheaton, Illinois, in a series of three consultations. Participants dealt with "The Church in Local Settings," "The Church in New Frontiers of Mission," and "The Church in Response to Human Need."

The 1982 Grand Rapids "Consultation on the Relation-

ship Between Evangelism and Social Responsibility"
(CRESR) was possibly the most significant of the two. It
produced a report intended to complete the unfinished
business of Lausanne 1974, which did not spell out the relationship of evangelism to social responsibility, except to
say that evangelism is primary.

The 1982 report noted that up to the nineteenth century, evangelism and social responsibility were intimately
related. During the first Great Awakening (1726-1750s)
and in other evangelical revivals in North America and Europe, there was no question about their interrelatedness.
Social concern was part of the task of evangelism. But as
the social gospel was developed by some theologians, with
the focus on the kingdom of God being built on the earth,
many evangelicals became suspicious and reacted negatively. This consultation now aimed to recapture what was
lost during the early part of this century.

The report contends that there are three equally valid
relationships between evangelism and social responsibility. First, social action is a *consequence* of evangelism; and
more than that, it is one of its principal aims, since Jesus
came to redeem us from all iniquity.

Second, social action is a *bridge* to evangelism. It opens
the door for a hearing of the gospel.

Third, social action does not only precede evangelism
and provide a bridge to evangelism, or follow evangelism
as a goal and consequence of evangelism. Much more, social action accompanies evangelism as its *partner*.

The report makes clear that social responsibility and
evangelism should not be identified with each other, yet
they involve each other. While they are distinct from one
another, they are integrally related in the proclamation of
the gospel and obedience to it. The partnership, it affirms,
is a *marriage*.

Regarding the issue of priority, the report holds that

evangelism has a *logical* priority, but not necessarily a *temporal* one. Sometimes social ministry will come first. However, "if social action is a consequence and aim of evangelism (as we have asserted), then evangelism must precede it" in rank (CRESR: 455). Since evangelism relates to the eternal destiny of people, it is of greater importance. Yet one seldom has to choose between the two. They are not competing; they are mutually supportive.

This position became more and more claimed by the church-growth movement in the 1980s. In his *Strategies for Church Growth*, Peter Wagner notes that there are five possible options in the debate over whether the social or cultural mandate claims priority, or whether the evangelistic mandate in missions takes primacy:

1. Mission involves the cultural mandate only; the program of mission must not be about proselyting persons of other faiths.

2. The cultural mandate takes priority over the evangelistic mandate.

3. Both mandates have equal weight, and they should not be prioritized.

4. The evangelistic mandate has priority over the cultural mandate.

5. Mission involves the evangelistic mandate only.

Wagner states that most evangelicals find themselves at position three, four, or five. But he feels that position four (giving priority to evangelism) is the most helpful for planning strategies for church growth. Thus it is a pragmatic position. However, Wagner also claims to hold this view not only because it is pragmatic but because he sees it as being biblical (102-103).

Wagner admits that there are cases when social ministries and evangelism have enjoyed a symbiotic relationship and helped each other. But in other cases, it has not worked out well and has actually hindered church growth.

"I'll grant," he says, "that there may be unusual circumstances in which, due to disastrous social conditions, the best Christian decision might be to reverse the priorities temporarily. But I am regarding this as an exception, not the rule" (108).

While the church-growth movement, though pressing ahead of earlier generations, was taking a more conservative stance, more-progressive evangelicals were developing leadership. Some such as Tom Sine, Ronald Sider, Howard Snyder, and Jim Wallis argued for broader social and political involvement. They were making a significant impact on the evangelical community.

Thus Jim Wallis wrote in the January 1, 1985, *Sojourners* that there was a rise of Christian conscience in social and political responsibility. He saw the churches in North America going through fundamental transformation, gaining a politically independent Christian conscience. It was neither right nor left, liberal nor conservative. Traditional labels and ideological categories no longer fit.

The 1990s

Even with Jim Wallis's optimism, the 1990s still found the evangelical community divided. In 1993 Ronald Sider argued that Christians have been one-sided. During the twentieth century, evangelicals for the most part have been strong on personal evangelism but without much passion for social justice. On the other hand, mainline churches have focused on peace and justice with little emphasis on personal evangelism, church growth, and cross-cultural sharing of their Christian faith.

With this "one-sided" Christianity, one group saves souls while the other reforms structures (Sider: 14-15, 25). But this division and dichotomizing of Christian outreach is not only between evangelicals and mainline churches; it continues to exist within evangelicalism.

Charles Van Engen rightly claims that the relation of personal salvation to social transformation is still not yet resolved (1990:232). We are at the turn of another century, and the debate continues. We search for new arguments, new methods, new ways of recapturing God's initial model. Van Engen insightfully suggests that "evangelicals have the possibility of developing a new concept of evangelism for the whole person that combines a deep spirituality with a concern for each individual's total welfare. "Third-world theologians, less affected by the old fundamentalist-modernist controversies, may be able to construct just such a synthesis" (1990:232).

In this book, I put together just such a synthesis. However, I intend not simply to base it upon a cultural two-thirds-world foundation, valuable as that may be. Instead, I will build it upon a foundation which is rooted in Scripture, particularly in the life and ministry of Jesus Christ. It will have a biblical and Christocentric basis.

2

Hermeneutical Method

When we speak of a "biblical basis" for evangelism, what do we really mean? All evangelicals ground their understanding of evangelism and their definition of the concept in the authority of the Scriptures. Yet as the history of the debate between fundamentalists and progressive evangelicals has shown, we still come out on different sides of the fence; some even straddle the fence.

Alfred Krass senses our dilemma and is convinced that we must develop a new understanding of how to read the Scriptures if we are to reach some missiological common ground. "We need to be more conscious of our hermeneutic and our way of interpreting Scripture" (93).

Many persons may challenge this, arguing that one needs no new hermeneutic. The Bible should be taken as it is. But that is simplistic. Scripture cannot be studied from a value-neutral or a purely historical point of view. We all bring our presuppositions to the texts. We apply our distinct perspective to the biblical material.

The only way we can truly hear the Word of God is if we are critical about our value judgments and ideas and our historical, theological, and even missiological presuppositions which we bring to the text. We seek a hermeneutic which will allow us to hear messages in Scripture that transcend any narrow individualistic understanding of evangelism.

As we attempt this task, we need take care that we do not fall in the rut of many before us. All Christian missiologists have looked to the Bible as a charter. It has often been apologetically and selectively used to underwrite certain strategies. Many of these single readings of Scripture have been myopic and self-serving.

For example, it is inadequate to read Luke-Acts as a document which prioritizes church planting, and yet ignore other New Testament testimonies. It is just as inadequate to read the classical prophets to buttress a social agenda if that is done at the expense of other dimensions of the evangelistic task (Senior: xi). Yet this is the very approach used uncritically during the past two centuries, in search of a biblical foundation for different strategies of mission and evangelism.

This uncritical selectivity is seen in the debate between those who view evangelism in personal terms, and those who see it more in social terms. Those who argue for the priority of personal salvation seek support in the great commission in Matthew (28:18-20), the opening lines of Acts (1:1-8), Paul's call for belief and verbal confession (Rom. 10), and similar texts. In so doing they may not really teach disciples to "obey everything" our Lord has commanded (Matt. 28:20) nor look at social transformation in the early church as portrayed in Acts and Paul's epistles.

Others turn to such passages as Luke 4 to ground their argument for a social component. Yet they may miss the need for the power and guidance of the Holy Spirit in believers and the call for true repentance and inner transformation.

Such selectivity has been detrimental to the evangelistic cause. Yet it may also be the salvation of the enterprise when critically applied to a text in sustained and fair study. This is what we hope to accomplish. But to outline this method, we must review the history of some other ways of reading Scripture and of viewing its inspiration and authority.

Competing Models

To a large extent, fundamentalists hold to an absolute inerrant view of the Bible's inspiration and authority. In the spectrum of the divine-human, they emphasize the divine aspect so strongly emphasized that the human is almost neglected.

Many subscribe to this fundamentalist model while affirming the divine authority of the total Scriptures. Yet they tend to elevate portions of the Bible to positions of authority, with more inspiration than others. This is demonstrated in the uses of the proof-text method: selected texts are pulled from here and there as inspired nuggets of truth to support a particular theological or missiological position. In this model, the Scripture is viewed as a religious encyclopedia of codes, information, and mandates.

As Glen Greenwalt has rightly pointed out, "[Rather] than being a book filled with a rich and wonderful diversity of literature—from stories, poetry, proverbs, and gospels, to parables, apocalyptic dramas, and even occasional fables, the Bible becomes a divinely appointed encyclopedia of information, or a code book of cultic and moral regulation" (3). Thus it has been traditional to elevate single passages, sentences, phrases, and words as direct communications from God in inflexible mandates that are eternal, nontemporal, and noncultural in their application.

We find this hermeneutic at work in the case of the relation of the New Testament with the Old Testament. Sometimes the New Testament is given uncritical preeminence over the Old. Even within the New Testament itself, many Protestants, following Luther's lead, have given Paul's theology a place of inspired honor not enjoyed by James. Thus they have a "canon within a canon."

The same is often done with the Gospels. Matthew's Gospel is treated (consciously or unconsciously) as more inspired and having more authority than, say, Luke's Gospel. Thus we see certain words of Jesus in Matthew 28 as taking precedence over his words in Luke 4.

If we treat some parts of the Scriptures as more inspired and authoritative than others, we are forced to posit a God who was more inspired on some occasions than on others (Birch: 145). Such a statement, of course, would be denied by those who hold to an inerrantist hermeneutic. Yet in the practical use of Scripture, this is what is affirmed.

In the nineteenth century, liberal theological thinkers sought to counteract the doctrine of inerrant inspiration and authority. They argued that it was not the words or sentences that were inspired but the thoughts and person of the biblical author. Writers chose their own style, words, and illustrations. "Their arguments are culture specific. Inspiration resides in the ideas conveyed" (Greenwalt: 4).

According to this approach, the Bible must be read against the religious and cultural background of each author. The reader seeks to understand not only what the writer was trying to say, but why and how it was being said. What matters is the direction toward which the authors were leading, not merely specific commands, codes, or mandates. What one seeks to find are the principles.

This hermeneutical model that looks at the Scriptures for inspired principles is superior in our opinion to the inerrant model. It recognizes and appreciates the diversity and varied texture of the biblical text. It allows flexibility in the use of the text, particularly for decision making in situations where there are no clear answers or direction for a contemporary reader.

However, there are a number of problems with the principle approach. Greenwalt raises several vital questions. "Why should we believe that the ideas of the biblical writer are more immune from the effects of historical conditioning than the words, sentences, illustrations, or method of argumentation?" (4-5). Also, how do we know what the principles are? There are many ambiguous texts which elicit varied interpretations. Will we need experts to articulate the principles?

In addition, when we have isolated the principle or varied principles, which one do we choose? On what basis does the reader claim supremacy of one principle over the other? Does the principle "Go and preach an individualistic personal salvation" take priority over the principle "Go and become a political and social liberator?"

Because of the problems of these text-based hermeneutical models, a reaction to them arose early in the twentieth century. In place of the inspiration and authority of the Bible residing in its content, Scripture was seen by many theologians as an encounter with God. Thus Karl Barth argued that it is not propositions or information or even principles that are revealed in revelation. Instead, God is revealed. "In revelation we are brought rather into a relationship with the person of God" (Greenwalt: 5).

Objections have been raised to the encounter hermeneutic. First, the notion of encountering God reinforces the notion (rooted in Protestantism) of an individualistic religion—a notion which many have shown to be unbiblical. Second, it is not clear how one encounters God in Scripture, or how God speaks to us through the Bible under this model so much better than under the others (Greenwalt: 6). Furthermore, how does this model give us a biblical grounding for the task of mission and evangelism?

According to Glen Greenwalt, a hermeneutical consensus is emerging which views the authority of Scripture in reference to its power to shape and form a particular way of life—both personal and communal (Greenwalt: 6). The stories, rules, codes, principles, commands, mandates, and admonitions—all are appropriated, and all participate in the shaping of life.

Walter Brueggemann uses this model of shaping a lifestyle when he proposes that evangelism is "doing the text again, as our text and as 'news' addressed to us and waiting to be received, appropriated, and enacted in our own time and place" (8). To "do the text" is to participate in and reenact the drama of the text.

But how does one "do the text"? How do we participate in the drama? We have to recognize that a distance exists between the world of the biblical writers and our world. We live in a new and different historical moment. Scripture can't simply be directly applied. The social situation in first-century Palestine, for example, and the forces at work then can't be directly equated with particular situations and forces today—even though there are closer equations in some areas than in others.

So we have to agree that the text cannot be reduced to "what it meant" and certainly not simply to "what it means"—to use Krister Stendhal's famous phrases. Instead, we agree with those who like David Bosch call for an approach that requires interaction between the "self-definition" of early Christian authors and actors, and today's Christians who wish to be inspired and guided by the former (Bosch, 1991:23; Greenwalt: 7-9). As we analyze the text and engage it, however, we must be suspicious of imposing a pet contemporary ideology upon the process (Krass: 98-100).

When one becomes immersed in this method, it soon becomes obvious that the Bible is not monolithic; it is multifaceted. Therefore, we must read each text and body of texts within their context, taking note of their various nuances (Van Engen, 1993b:28). We will, therefore, engage different texts, passages, and books differently—hearing each uniquely, and appropriating each uniquely as well.

We will not succumb to the temptation of taking some parts of the Scriptures more seriously than other parts, nor upholding one imperative over another, nor selecting a "canon within a canon" (Birch: 156-158). Instead, we recognize that the context, the audience, and the missionary concerns of different authors all have validity. Each can speak to us today with equal power.

A Contextual Model

Earlier we spoke about a hermeneutical approach which requires interacting "self-definitions" between the biblical author and the contemporary reader and interpreter. With regard to this, David Bosch argues that we have to admit that self-definitions might be wrong and inadequate; so they need to be subject to criticism and challenge. There is no "objective reality" when it comes to our self-definition.

If reality changes, one's self-definition changes. This is just as true for the early Christians as it is for us now. As time passed, the self-definitions of those Christians changed; and their lives, writings, and mission changed in relation to these new definitions (Bosch, 1991:24).

Students of the New Testament have recognized in recent decades that not only were self-definitions and outlooks changing. In addition, various segments of the early Christian communities had different self-definitions and varied ideological perspectives. As the contexts of these communities differed, so did the ministry to them by their leaders and apostles.

Today we understand the ministry and mission of the leaders through the varied documents of the New Testament. Each biblical work represents the theological and missiological position of the author and possibly reflects the unique life-situation of the receivers. In this critical area of study, one is concerned with the theological motivation of an author who collects, arranges, edits, and modifies the received material. In doing so, the author creates and composes new material which represents the new self-definition. This, says Norman Perrin, (1969:1) could be called "composition criticism" because it is concerned with the composition of new material and arranging of redacted or newly created or existing material.

The evangelical student of the New Testament does not deny the basic involvement of the Holy Spirit in the process; but there is an affirmation of human process at work, cooperating with the divine. A careful analysis of the Gospel writers, for example, demonstrates that each play ed creative roles; they interpreted and they modified.

Each author of a Gospel was interpreting and modifying the material of Jesus and about Jesus and his movement. While so doing, each evangelist reveals something about his own theological peculiarities and evangelistic purpose for that one's contextual situation. Their dogmatic, theological, and missiological conceptions were at work in their unique, inspired creations.

The Gospel writers were not scholars doing systematic research, however. They wrote in the context of situations in which they were forced to theologize by grappling with the mission at hand. Because each situation was different, each document was different; each theology and missiology was different. So in reality there is not one theology of mission or evangelism in the Gospel, but a variety of theologies of mission and evangelism.

When we consider Luke, we recognize that Hans Conzelmann's *Theology of St. Luke* (1960) was seminal in this area of study. This work produced a paradigm shift in our understanding of the Evangelists who wrote the four Gospels. Previously, Luke was regarded as the historian of early Christianity. But Conzelmann's work changed this understanding by portraying Luke the theologian.

All of Luke's geography, historical, and other references were controlled by his theology regarding the history of salvation (Perrin: 29). Others since Conzelmann have suggested additional theological motifs around which Luke structured his work. But it is widely agreed that he researched, redacted, and composed his two volumes with a particular theology and missionary purpose in mind (Keck; Rice; Verkuyl: 110).

Hence, Luke was a theologian and missiologist confronted with problems and self-definitions that were different from those faced by his contemporaries or his predecessors. This does not mean that he changed the basic Christian theology or broke with the original message. It simply means that he focused his narrative to meet the particular challenge faced by his community.

The observant reader of any synopsis of the Gospels will readily recognize minor and major differences in the records. Let's illustrate.[1] The introductory statement for each Gospel is different: Matthew begins with an edited genealogy which focuses on David and generations grouped in sets of fourteen (the numerical sum of the Hebrew consonants in the name *David*). Mark, in typical summary style, has no long genealogy but begins with a simple sentence: "The beginning of the good news of Jesus Christ, the Son of God" (1:1).

Luke, on the other hand, is the only evangelist to do a scholarly job of first laying out his method of investigation and composition in the creation of these theological volumes. John begins with a prologue which sets up his presupposition regarding the preexistence and incarnation of Jesus Christ. Each of these beginnings are deliberately and strategically placed there in order to lay a groundwork for the theological trajectory of the rest of the Gospel.

The differences and the independent unique focus of each author is also demonstrated in how they each begin Jesus' Galilean ministry with a different major event. For Matthew, it is the Sermon on the Mount (5–7); Luke places this later in his Gospel and presents it as the Sermon on a Level Place (6:17-49). Mark begins the Galilean ministry with the healing of the man with an unclean spirit at the synagogue and his confrontation with the demons (1:21-28).

Luke introduces the Galilean ministry with Jesus' visit to the synagogue at Nazareth and the announcement of his mission—what his messiahship was all about (4:16-30). John starts with the wedding at Cana of Galilee—the first of only seven signs or miracles which he records Jesus as doing (2:1-11).

Suppose the authors were simply recording eyewitness history or writing a biographical account of the life and ministry of Jesus. Then we might expect at least some basic agreement between them as to this most significant event, the beginning of his ministry. But they were not writing a biography or a history of Jesus. They only utilized history and biography to present and illustrate their theological focus.

To illustrate this more precisely, note the birth narratives recorded in Matthew and Luke, the only two Gospels which find them essential to their theological emphases. Many recognize that Matthew is interested in the issue of kingship; Luke is not. Luke highlights ordinary people, the marginal, the unexpected. Hence, Matthew's genealogy is radically different from Luke's. Matthew focuses on David and his royal lineage. Luke has been thought for centuries to give Mary's ancestry, though no one is sure. Be that as it may, Matthew's birth narrative highlights Joseph, while Luke's centers around Mary.

In Matthew, the first appearance of the angel is to Joseph to announce that Jesus is the child conceived by Mary. In Luke, however, Mary is the one to whom the angel appears and announces that the child in her womb is Jesus. In Matthew, Mary is hardly mentioned, and when she is, it is only secondarily. In Luke, she is the center of the narrative. In addition to the visit of the angel Gabriel, Mary has a significant visit with Elizabeth, she sings a major song of praise, and she receives a special prophetic word from old Simeon in the temple; none of this is recorded by Matthew.

Matthew, on the other hand, concentrates on royalty and persons of higher status. Besides the birth narratives centering around Joseph, Matthew has the first announcement about the birth of the child being made to the wise men from the East—wealthy persons. They bring treasure chests which include gold, frankincense, and myrrh. These wise men first visit a king, Herod, a figure on whom Matthew zeros in. When Herod threatens the life of the child, the family flees to a rival realm, Egypt, and does not return until there is a new ruler in Judea.

Luke's theological purpose ignores much of this and does not include any of the stories in Matthew. Instead, his narratives center on the lowly and the despised. The announcement of the birth is made to the shepherds who are keeping watch over their sheep at night. They seek out no royal palace; instead, they go directly to the manger; Matthew says nothing about such a humble place; he has the baby in a house when the wise men arrive. And when it is time for the blessing of the child, Luke does not provide priests and mighty ones to invoke God's blessing; instead, two unknowns appear, Simeon and Anna.

In the next chapter, we demonstrate how Luke's portrayal of John the Baptist's evangelism differs from that of Matthew's. Luke reflects his special missiological paradigm. In Matthew, John calls for repentance because "the kingdom of heaven has come near" (3:2); in Luke, the Baptist makes no such reference to the kingdom.

Matthew's stress on the kingdom is seen also in the temptation narrative. Traditionally, many have assumed that the sequence of Jesus' temptations in Matthew is chronological. We have ignored the fact that Luke presents them in a different order. Matthew's theological perspective highlights rulership and realm. This leads him to place last, as a climax, the temptation regarding the kingdoms of the world (4.8-10). Such a position would not fit into Luke's theology about the low and the marginal. Instead, that temptation about the kingdoms is placed in the middle, the place of least significance in Greek rhetoric (4:5-8).

Each evangelist is a creative author, theologian, and missiologist. He is selecting, editing, and arranging the material to fit a particular worldview and self-definition. This is a unique missiological task. So none of the Gospel records can be called *the* normative recital of the good news. Each one is *a* recital of the Gospel as relevant to a particular time, situation, and community. Each retelling is an imaginative witness of the author's understanding of mission and evangelism at that time and in that place.

We therefore err when we attempt to hold up one biblical book or text as the supreme guide and mandate for mission and evangelism. Every book and every text is supremely valuable if we allow each to be read on its own terms. Beverly Gaventa supports this position, claiming that the text needs to be read as inductively as possible. It should be read "from the inside." Instead of seeking isolated texts, "we need to ask what the dynamics of the text are: That is, what does the text wish to say, and how is that conveyed?" (414). When such questions are asked of a particular book or text, we are less likely to set up priorities in the missiological enterprise.

In the next two chapters, we listen to Luke, hearing his special inspired theology and description of evangelism as portrayed in his major work. We will follow the hermeneutical method of hearing a particular book and its theology and missiology. This, however, is not to deny the larger hermeneutical approaches which look at missiological themes throughout the Scriptures and create a tapestry from which we can extrapolate for the contemporary scene.[2]

The method we are using, rather, simply alerts us to the too-often-ignored fact that God speaks to us differently and specifically (Heb. 1:1). Our missionary and evangelistic task can be enhanced and gain in integrity when we recognize that a multiplex approach to the task is infinitely superior to the traditional narrow one.

3

Reading Luke-Acts Again

To hear Luke's unique word on evangelism, we must first decipher the concept of evangelism presented in his two-volume work. We will compare that with popular definitions of the term.

Defining Evangelism

In the traditional definition, *evangelism* means "to proclaim the good news." The words *evangelism* or *evangelization* do not occur as such in the New Testament. Yet these modern terms are derived from Greek words associated with "good news" and its proclamation or announcement. Thus Walter Brueggemann can declare that at the center of evangelism is "the message announced, a verbal, out-loud assertion of something decisive not known until the moment of utterance" (14).

The Greek words behind this concept of evangelism are derived from the noun *euangelion* (good news, gospel) and its verbal cognate, *euangelizō/euangelizomai* (I proclaim good news). David Barrett (10-14) says these terms occur twenty-five times in the Greek Old Testament (LXX), with the basic meaning of carrying or bringing good news.

In the New Testament, these words are used over 130 times.[1] The verb forms used in the Gospels refer to the earthly ministry and activity of Jesus, proclaiming the arrival of the kingdom. This, according to Barrett, is unique to the pre-resurrection ministry of Jesus and does not refer directly to the activity of the early Christians after that ministry. The new gospel proclaimed by the apostles is that Christ was raised from the dead. Although Barrett focuses his definition of this Greek stem on proclamation, he does see hints that it has a more wide-ranging and all-inclusive meaning.

More scholars are recognizing that the traditional definition of proclamation is inadequate and that no one word fully captures the concept (Abraham: 40; Green: 48). In the first place, other terms are used to convey the concept; one such is the word *witness*. David Bosch points out that this noun occurs thirteen times in Acts, and only once in Luke's Gospel; but it is in one of the most important passages, Luke 24:48 (1991:116). Bosch counts *witness* as a crucial term for mission in Luke.

It seems that *apostle* and *witness* are practically synonymous (see Acts 1:2, 8; 10:41; 13:31). *Witness* is applied to others such as Stephen and Paul (Acts 22:15, 20; 26:16). And in Acts 1:22, one of the characteristics of the new apostle was to be a witness to the resurrection.

In this dimension of evangelism, witness to Jesus is required. Of course, witness of the passion events is most important. This is a point also emphasized in Luke—"Thus it is written, that the Messiah is to suffer and to rise from the dead on the third day, and that repentance and forgiveness of sins is to be proclaimed in his name to all nations. . . . You are witnesses of these things" (24:46-48).

However, it is more even than that. The term *Messiah* is mentioned in the passage. In selection of the new apostle, it was agreed to select someone who had accompanied Jesus from John's baptism until the resurrection. All this shows that the whole ministry of Christ was included in the witness. The whole life of Christ was vital to early Christian theology and missiology. Why else would they write the Gospels, and multiple perspectives at that? (Green: 72).

The definition of evangelism which focuses on proclamation and particularly on *euangelizō* continues to dominate the evangelical scene. Barrett, in chapter 7 of his book *Evangelize! A Historical Survey of the Concept*, discusses scores of synonyms for the word (15-19). But they are all terms which either focus on preaching and proclamation, or on evangelism to individuals. The reason for this narrow focus seems partly to be the presupposition that the first part of the Matthean great commission is the defining text for evangelism.[2] Even though the great commission does not have the word *euangelizō*, it is understood as the only grounding for the enterprise. Thus Barrett's book, like so many similar ones, is colored by this presupposition and understanding of evangelism.

However, such a limited way of reading Scripture is inadequate. It is not right to use Acts as the primary interpreter of Matthew, or to let Matthew define the Lukan understanding of evangelism in Acts. It is faulty hermeneutical gymnastics to leap from Matthew to Acts without taking note of their different theological and missiological foci. As shown in the previous chapter (above), Luke and Matthew have different perspectives. We need to hear each separately. Furthermore, we must recapture Luke's perspective which was lost with the hellenization of Christianity.[3]

In word study it is important to remember that terms should be understood in their context. James Barr in *The Semantics of Biblical Language* (1961) has alerted us to the inadequacies of using linguistic evidence in theological discussions. He has argued forcefully that theological super-structures should not be built upon particular words. Thus concordances and even studies in theological word dictionaries have their limitations.[4] Therefore, valuable as they may be, word studies which attempt to fix a definition of evangelism come up short.

In recent years, more interpreters are taking the view that the mission and evangelistic task of Jesus fits no prescribed formula, no "clearly circumscribable framework" (Bosch, 1991:47). His evangelism was situational and not propositional. There is no one pattern. Jesus used a pluralistic approach (Krass: 111). It was a "polymorphous" activity (Abraham: 104).

To limit Jesus' ministry to proclamation is reductionist. The activities of Jesus, the apostles in the primitive church, and even persons like Philip and Paul—all demonstrate that the evangelistic task cannot be so limited. When this is recognized, one may conclude that it is difficult to say what an evangelist was in the early church (Abraham: 51-52). But this is not really so if one has a wholistic view of evangelism, one which rejects dividing evangelism into three parts: pre-evangelism, evangelism, and post-evangelism.

Van Engen counsels us not to separate "the matters of the church's presence in the world (pre-evangelism), along with incorporation of the converts into the church (follow-up or post-evangelism), [and treat them] as somehow different from the events of the communication of the Gospel itself (evangelism)" (1992:76). Luke's evangelism is whole.

Luke presents Jesus' evangelistic activities as preaching and healing, teaching and acting. "The Eternal Word-became-Flesh was the perfect combination of word and deed" (Sider: 72). And the mandate of the early church, according to Acts, was not limited to proclamation and witness. It included transforming actions on the part of followers of the Way. "We find no dichotomy between word and deed in the church's witness, no splitting of proclamation from demonstration" (Van Engen, 1992:88).

Hence, this hackneyed business about a dichotomy between social action and evangelism is fundamentally misguided, according to Brueggemann (1993:43). It is difficult to find a foundation for it anywhere in Scripture, and it is totally absent in Luke. Thus Beverly Gaventa says,

> Much conversation in the church today presupposes a distinction between personal salvation and social justice, thus the discussions of wholistic conversion and wholistic mission. This dichotomy is of course a false one. Luke is so comfortable with the personal and corporate dimensions of Christian proclamation that I wonder how and why we have introduced the dichotomy. Luke understands, as do all New Testament writers, that belief and action are two parts of one entity, and his clarity causes me to be amazed at our attempt to divide the indivisible. (424)

In part, the answer to Gaventa's wonder is found in the pervasive influence of individualism, particularly in the West. "The ideologies of individualism are certainly at variance with the biblical understanding of salvation. In Scripture, personal realities are never divorced from social and historical realities" (Wallis, 1976:30).

Therefore, what we call "evangelism" and "social action or concern" belong together. "Jesus' evangelization was not limited to 'saving souls' or to what we anachronistically might call 'social services' " (Arias: 3). Michael Green correctly observes, "It would be unthinkable that Jesus should have preached but not healed; or that he should have fed the multitude but given no indication of where the Bread of Life might be found. The two are inseparable" (56).

Thus evangelism is rightly a "polymorphous" activity which should not be dichotomized. It has its anchor in the person and mission of Jesus. The first word on evangelism must be how "Jesus and his followers conceived and carried out the first, and paradigmatic, evangelistic actions of the church" (Abraham: 17). This is what Luke is attempting to do in his theological and missiological reflections in his two-volume work. Here we find evangelism fitting the definition of both William Abraham (13) and Walter Brueggemann (10-11); it is an invitation into the reign of God and an initiation into that reign—a reign that impacts all contemporary living, private and public, without ignoring the future eschatological dimension.

Trajectory Through Luke-Acts

The evangelistic mission in Luke could, with some justification, be viewed as three-pronged: first, the empowering of the weak and lowly; second, the healing of the sick; and third, the saving of the lost. However, David Bosch warns us to be careful in making such precise divisions. Luke's material defies such neat categorization. "Luke did not understand Jesus' ministry as consisting of three separate activities, but as one multifaceted response to *suffering*" (1989:4-5). Though the divisions help us distinguish between the major thrusts of his ministry, we must not isolate them from each other, Bosch says.

This principle of unity and yet division for the sake of discussion and clarity is handy. However, instead of a three-pronged approach, we propose that Luke's evangelism functions in a double way: Hope and Challenge. It brings good news and hope to the marginal and outcast, a message of liberation and redemption. But this redeeming evangelism is also a challenge to the powerful and those who reject the call to repentance. In that case, it becomes bad news of judgment.

On one hand, evangelism communicates the good news that new life is possible. The reign of God is inaugurated. All are invited to be citizens and children of God. On the other hand, it is an all-out attack on all manifestations of evil, such as pain, sickness, death, all types of social and personal sins, and all brokenness in human relationships (Castro: 88; Bosch, 1991:32-33).

Luke illustrates his approach best through his interest in the poor and other marginalized groups. They head the list of categories of people prominent in the two volumes. On the other hand, the rich and powerful are challenged the most. Hence, there is evangelism to the poor, those who need hope, who need to hear the good news. And there is evangelism to the rich, those who are challenged to change their ways, particularly with regard to their treatment of the weak, oppressed, and marginal.

Hope

Luke is particularly interested in the social well-being of the poor. This is seen in his redaction of material as he researched, edited, and compiled it into his theological framework. Several passages are unique to his Gospel: Mary's Magnificat, in which the hungry are filled and the rich are sent away empty (1:53); Jesus' Sermon on the Level Place, giving blessing for the poor and a curse for the rich (6:20, 24); the parables of the rich fool (12:16-21), and the rich man and Lazarus (16:19-31); and the conversion of Zacchaeus, the chief tax collector of Jericho.

Early in his Gospel, Luke also edits the tradition regarding John the Baptist so that it focuses on the socioeconomic dimension. In addition, Luke uses the word *ptōchos* (poor) ten times in his Gospel, compared to five times each in Matthew and Mark. He uses numerous other words for want and need, and various terms referring to wealth and possessions (Bosch, 1991:98).

In the previous chapter (above), we noted that Luke's narrative of the birth of Jesus differs markedly from Matthew's in its focus on the marginal within society. It is to the poor that angels appear with good news; to such the announcement of salvific hope is given.

The narrative of the virgin Mary stands at a place of prominence in Luke. She's a woman, a virgin, one of the weak and poor. Yet the angel appears to her and says, "Greetings, favored one! The Lord is with you" (1:28). She is promised that the son she will conceive will be great (1:32). The reversal motif has begun to be played out.

However, it is in Mary's song of praise, the Magnificat, that this comes to full bloom. Luke 1:51-53 contains the most powerful language of the poem and brings it to a climax (see Tannehill, 1986:28). The words are strong, graphic, and emphatic; as the pace of the poem quickens, Luke eliminates all articles and most conjunctions. God's reversal of the existing order is stated in strong language, full of sharp reversals—reversals which not only bring down the powerful, but bring fulfilled hope to the weak:

> [The Lord] has shown strength with his arm;
>> he has scattered the proud in the thoughts of their
>> hearts.
> He has brought down the powerful from their
>> thrones,
>> and lifted up the lowly;
> he has filled the hungry with good things,
>> and sent the rich away empty. (1:51-53)

These poetic words at the beginning of Luke's two volumes anticipate Jesus' words of comfort to the poor and weak. "This social reversal which Mary celebrates will be realized concretely through Jesus' ministry and through his witnesses who continue to 'upset the world' (Acts 17:6)" (Tannehill, 1986:28). Tannehill also shows us that God's intervention for the humble and poor in general indicates that his grace to this humble girl, Mary, is an "emblem or paradigm" of his saving work which was beginning (1986:29).

Luke continues to make his point forcefully in his unique Christmas drama, with the story of the shepherds and their visit from the angel (2:8-20). The shepherds represent the marginalized and disinherited, without hope and filled with despair. They are visited by an angel who tells them, "Do not be afraid; for see—I am bringing you good news of great joy for all the people" (2:10). In parallel with the angel's words to Mary, the multitude of heavenly hosts join this angel, praising God and saying,

> Glory to God in the highest heaven,
>   and on earth peace among those whom *he favors!*
> (2:14)

This account, says Brueggemann, "is positioned in the gospel story to initiate the much larger account of healing power unleashed in the Lukan narrative. The gospel announced by the angels and received by the shepherds reverberates among many people who also have their lives dislocated" (34).

The same reversal motif which demonstrates the evangelism of hope in the Mary and shepherd narratives is also picked up in Simeon's words (2:34). He prophesies that Jesus is the one who will cause "the falling and the rising of many in Israel."

Jesus' statement in Luke 4:18-19 is the defining passage in the Lukan evangelistic program. Those who focus on the personal, proclamative aspect of evangelism use the great commission of Matthew as their programmatic battle cry. Those who focus on social action and concern elevate this passage from Luke. Neither text is *the* only biblical word on evangelism. Yet it cannot be denied that for Luke, this section is unquestionably most important. The entire pericope of 4:16-30 serves as a programmatic discourse. It has the same function for Luke as the Sermon on the Mount does for Matthew (Bosch, 1991:89).

Luke alone records this Nazareth episode, strategically placing it at the beginning of Jesus' public ministry. His ministry must be interpreted in light of it (Tannehill, 1986:61). Matthew strategically places the great commission at the end of his Gospel as an important closure to his theological focus. Likewise, Luke has this manifesto concerning Jesus' mission at the beginning to alert the reader to the nature of Luke's theology of evangelism and mission. In it, Luke portrays the nature of the salvation that Jesus brings (Dyrness: 150). It is a particular understanding of God's salvific program for which Jesus is the Messiah, for which he was anointed as king.

The Luke 4:18-21 discourse highlights one of the central themes of Luke: Jesus fulfills the Old Testament promises by offering salvation to the marginal and those without hope. The reading of Isaiah 61:1-2 as Jesus' first public act is no happenstance for Luke. It is foundational for his missiology.

Jesus begins by declaring himself Messiah in his admission that he has been anointed to bring good news. Traditionally, messiahship and good news (gospel) have been linked only to the cross and personal salvation and a particular understanding of the atonement. Luke's theology has another track. For him, the Messiah and the gospel are associated with the poor.

Because this is such an obvious fact, many have sought

to get around such an understanding by interpreting "the poor" and other categories in the passage metaphorically. We will not deny that the terms could be extended to have a metaphorical range. But if we limit them to that, or make such meaning take precedence over the physical and socioeconomic sense, then we do injustice to Luke's intent. For Luke, as throughout Scripture, the poor first of all are persons without economic resources (Maynard-Reid, 1987). They are the ones given good news and hope, and they receive special attention in Luke's evangelistic program.

Immediately following the reference to the poor is the announcement that Jesus is sent to proclaim release to the captives. There is a growing consensus that these two lines ("good news to the poor," and "release to the captives") may be synonymous. Thus the captives would chiefly be those economically oppressed and enslaved by debts (see Tannehill, 1986:65).

However, because "release" is central to Luke's theology, we might well understand the phrase to have a wider reference to enslavement other than debtors in prison. It may also refer to persons held captive by demonic possession and by physical ailments due to demonic activity. This discourse is followed by accounts of Jesus casting the spirit of an unclean demon out of a man (4:33-36) and healing Simon's mother of a fever which appears to have been caused by a demon (4:38-39). Luke may have had this dimension in mind as he gave prominence to Isaiah when Jesus reads the Scripture.[5]

The third phrase in the outline of Jesus' mission is "the recovery of sight to the blind." Here again, if we are going to be faithful to Luke's missiology, we have to interpret it in literal, physical terms. However, Robert Tannehill has shown that this could also be referring to Jesus' entire task of healing.[6] Blindness as an ailment is one type of physical problem which could stand for all (1986:66). As in the case of "the poor," so also "the blind" could be taken metaphorically for a lack of "perception of divine revelation and salvation" (1986:67; cf. Acts 28:26-27). Yet such a metaphorical interpretation must not be allowed to dilute Luke's intention in this context, where the sociophysical well-being of the whole person is paramount.

The next to last phrase, "to let the oppressed go free," is not in the original of Isaiah 61:1-2. Luke seems to have inserted this phrase from elsewhere in Isaiah:

> Is not this the fact that I choose:
>   to loose the bonds of injustice,
>   to undo the thongs of the yoke,
> *to let the oppressed go free*,
>   and to break every yoke? (58:6).

This Isaiah passage is unquestionably social in its intent. It is in the context of prophetic criticism of social abuses in Judah and the oppression of the poor by the rich (Bosch, 1991:100). Therefore, it is certain that Luke wants us to read this passage in socioeconomic and sociophysical categories. He wants his readers to realize that Jesus' mission is one which has a strong social component.

The programmatic statement ends as it began with a promised announcement: "to proclaim the year of the Lord's favor." As in Isaiah 61, this phrase is intended to assure the disappointed that "God has not forgotten them, but would come to their aid by ushering in 'the year of the Lord's favor,' namely the Jubilee" (Bosch, 1991:100).

Some interpreters question whether Luke has a Jubilee connection in mind. It is clear to all that this "year of the Lord's favor" is a time of salvation characterized by good news for the poor, blind, oppressed, and captives. It is also accepted that in Isaiah 61:1-2 there is a Jubilee connection.

However, Tannehill is among those who argue that the connection in Luke has not been convincingly proved, though it remains a possibility. "This is not to deny," he says, "that the social concern expressed in the Jubilee law is also present in Luke, for the 'good news to the poor' does reflect a concern for economic justice" (1986:68).[7]

Others are more convinced of the connection between "the year of the Lord's favor" and the ancient Jubilee year mandate of Leviticus 25. Tom Sine (32) sees it as outlining principles of the Jubilee year: every fifty years all slaves were to be freed, debts canceled, and land returned to its original owner. It was a day when justice would come.

Thus in his sermon on the Isaiah text, Jesus was saying that in him the Jubilee had arrived: "Today this scripture has been fulfilled in your hearing" (Luke 4:21). He was the good news to the poor, he was the harbinger of the new age of justice for the poor and the marginal. It would be an age in which "love would triumph over greed, light over darkness, freedom over enslavement, and hope over despair. Jesus was announcing the birth of a just and peaceful world" (Costas: 70). By beginning Jesus' ministry with these words, Luke introduces a theological motif of hope for the marginal ones who would be initiated into the reign of God.

The saying of Jesus in the Nazareth narrative is fulfilled in Luke's version of Matthew's Sermon on the Mount (Luke 6:17-49). Here Luke has Jesus coming down from the mountain to a level place. This is an important redaction for Luke's theology. Jesus is not upon a mountain above the crowds; he is down with the powerless, the sick, the oppressed, the marginal. This is the place where he preaches the gospel—the good news to the poor:[8]

> Blessed are you who are poor,
>   for yours is the kingdom of God. (6:20)

Here Jesus assures the poor of inheritance in the reign of God. It is a reign (as we will see later) that is not merely a future eschatological hope; it is also a present reality.

The present realization of the hope is seen in the discourse regarding the disciples of John and Jesus in Luke 7. John summoned two of his disciples and sent them to ask Jesus: "Are you the one who is to come, or are we to wait for another?" (7:18-23). Jesus responds to this messianic query by first curing many people of diseases, plagues, and evil spirits, and giving sight to many who were blind.

Then in a rhythmic series of brief sentences, he sends this message to John: "Go and tell John what you have seen and heard: the blind receive their sight, the lame walk, the lepers are cleansed, the deaf hear, the dead are raised, the poor have good news brought to them." This final phrase is a summary of all the manifestations of the reign of God in what Jesus had done; it also is a fleshing out of Jesus' salvific program of evangelism as outlined in his Nazareth declaration. It is a celebration of salvation! (Tannehill, 1986:79).

In the parabolic genre, the motif of hope for the socially marginal is also highlighted uniquely by Luke. First, the parable of the great dinner in 14:15-24 illustrates Jesus' mission to poor, physically challenged, and outcast. These are contrasted with the wealthy—"your friends or your brothers or your relatives or rich neighbors" (14:12). The marginal in the parable are described as persons who "cannot repay you" (14:14).

According to the Dead Sea Scrolls, such marginal persons like simpletons, or persons blind, maimed, lame, paralyzed, or deaf were excluded from the community.[9] In contrast, Jesus has the master of the house inviting such people to the table after the rich and powerful have refused. He tells his servant: "Go out at once into the streets and lanes of the town and bring in the poor, the crippled, the blind, and the lame" (14:21). Jesus directly instructs his hearers to do just that (14:13). This dinner represents the reign of God to which the marginal and outcasts are invited. Like Luke 4:18 and 6:20, this banquet portrays the gospel, the good news for the poor.

The triple parables of Luke 15 have traditionally been used to illustrate a personalized and individualistic salvation and an evangelistic call to such. We take no issue with any who would extrapolate from these parables a spiritual seeking and searching for the lost in terms of a future personal salvation. However, the Lukan context belies the fact that this is Luke's primary contention here. Luke 15:1-2 is the setting for the parable:

> Now all the tax collectors and sinners were coming near to listen to [Jesus]. And the Pharisees and the scribes were grumbling and saying, "This fellow welcomes sinners and eats with them."

Although the term "sinners" can be taken literally, in a context like this when it is associated with outcasts like prostitutes and tax collectors and the marginal, it should likely be interpreted in its social sense. It refers to how such persons are perceived by the powerful in society and the temple.[10] Except for Jesus, these lost people have no hope. He has found them; he gives them the good news of unconditional acceptance; he associates with them and eats with them. It is the celebration of the messianic banquet, because the lost and hopeless have been found.[11]

The seeking and saving of the lost—the outcast—is also highlighted in the narrative of Zacchaeus in Luke 19:1-10. The final statement in this account (also unique to Luke) makes the story a key example of Jesus' evangelistic enterprise: "For the Son of Man came to seek out and to save the lost" (19:10). His mission is concerned with seeking, saving, and restoring the outcast, the oppressed, the excluded.

This statement, says Tannehill, "also invites us to reread the story of Zacchaeus not as a story of Zacchaeus seeking Jesus, but as a story of Jesus seeking Zacchaeus, since that is what 'the Son of Man came' to do" (1986:125).

The motif of the gospel as good news for the poor seems to have run dry in Luke's second volume, says David Bosch (1991:104). Acts has it nowhere in the speeches of Peter, Stephen, and Paul. The word *ptōchos* (poor) does not appear in Acts! But this must be understood in the context of salvation in Luke-Acts. As we demonstrate below, the concept is comprehensive in both volumes. In the Gospel it certainly has a strong social and economic undertone. Yet, by the practice and lifestyle of the primitive church, it is obvious that the hope motif for the poor has not run dry.

This church was countercultural in its community life: sharing together, breaking down racial and cultural barriers which existed in Roman society (Sine: 40). Such a life demonstrated that the good news of the reign of God had truly been realized. "They made the grace of God credible by a society of love and mutual care which astonished the pagans and was recognized as something entirely new. It lent persuasiveness to their claim that the New Age had dawned in Christ" (Green: 120). In Acts, the good news for the poor is done in *deeds* along with being spoken in *words*.

There is one category of persons who should be given special notice. Luke, unlike any other New Testament or biblical author, singles them out as a distinctive part of his theology. In Luke's two volumes, women are clearly among the marginal to whom the gospel of hope is proclaimed.[12] To show the significance of this, Ronald Sider (66) summarizes their situation in first-century Palestine:

In Jesus' day, it was a scandal for a man to appear in public with a woman. A woman's word was considered useless in court. It was better to burn a copy of the Torah (the first five books of the Old Testament) than to allow a woman to touch it. Indeed, according to one first-century statement, "If any man teach his daughter Torah, it is as though he taught her lechery." Women were excluded from most parts of the temple. Nor did they count in calculating the quorum needed for a meeting in the synagogue. The Jewish prayer "I thank Thee, Lord, that Thou has not made me a Gentile, . . . a slave, . . . a woman" . . . is not a joke. First-century Jewish men regularly thanked God that they were not Gentiles, slaves, or women.

Luke challenges this status quo.

We already noted that Luke's birth narrative differs from Matthew's in its emphasis on Mary rather than Joseph. She is the one to whom the angel Gabriel announces the birth of the Messiah. Also, Luke parallels Mary with Matthew's Zechariah in angelic communication scenes (1:5-38). Luke has a similar parallel in the temple scene with Anna and Simeon (2:25-38). This inclusion of Anna demonstrates conclusively Luke's desire to balance a man with a woman. It reinforces Luke's pattern of referring to women as prophets, and to women as empowered to speak for God (as shown below).

In the Gospel of Luke, there is a distinct intent to enhance the position of women in a male-dominated society by using them as illustrations. In 4:20-30, right after Jesus' statement of his mission, the congregation is upset over the words of grace coming from his mouth. His hearers notice that he has stopped reading Isaiah 61:1-2 just before its mention of "the day of vengeance of our God."

The congregation is debating over who Jesus was,

making such a messianic claim of mercy offered now and through himself. In reply, Jesus uses the belief and cleansing of a Gentile leper, Naaman. But first he upholds a woman as a model, the widow at Zarephath, who accepted the prophet Elijah. After these illustrations, the crowd is enraged and leads Jesus to the brow of a hill, intending to dispose of him! They could not handle his elevation of a woman and a sick foreigner as good examples of faith and of accepting a prophet of the Lord.

In other passages, Jesus uses women as models and thus enhances their status. One of these is Luke 11:31-32. "The queen of the South will rise at the judgment with the people of this generation and condemn them, because she came from the ends of the earth to listen to the wisdom of Solomon." This queen is paralleled with the people of Nineveh who repented at the proclamation of Jonah.

Lukan parables also highlight women. In Luke 13:18-21 the mustard seed parable is paired with the parable of the yeast, in which a woman is engaged in the domestic duties of making bread. And in 15:4-10, the parable of the shepherd finding the sheep is alongside one of a woman seeking for and finding a coin; both shepherd and woman represent the God who searches for the lost and finds them!

Finally, in the eschatological discourse of Luke 17:20-37, Jesus ends with a focus on women by way of illustration. He said, "I tell you, on that night there will be two in one bed; one will be taken and the other left [masculine pronouns]. There will be two women grinding meal together; one will be taken and the other left" (17:35-36). In all these passages, Luke has women alongside men, thus emphasizing their similarity and equality.

In the healing stories, women are also prominent and parallel with men. A pair of healings illustrate Jesus' mission to bring release to those who are captive. The first subject is a man with an unclean spirit (4:31-37), but the second is a woman, Simon's mother-in-law, who was healed of their demonic fever (4:38-39). Also, following the healing of the centurion's servant (7:1-10), Jesus performs an even greater miracle, the raising of the widow's son at Nain (7:11-17).

Luke interrupts the story of Jarius and his sick and soon-to-die daughter. In the middle of this account, he creatively places the incident with the woman hemorrhaging for twelve years (8:40-56). Finally, the two Sabbath healings of 13:10-17 and 14:1-6 form a pair. In one case, Jesus heals a woman crippled for eighteen years. In the other, he cures a man who has dropsy. With all these parallels, Luke has Jesus showing that women also share equally in the reign of God.

In the story of Mary and Martha in 10:38-42, Mary is affirmed because she has taken on the role of a disciple at Jesus' feet. For Luke, the challenge of discipleship belongs to women as well as men. Women are not restricted to their roles as wives and mothers; they can be free from their domestic duties to follow the path of discipleship. In this narrative, Mary abandons her traditional role in the kitchen so she can listen to a theology lesson given by Jesus; and he defends her!

However, even when women are performing their traditional roles, Luke elevates them, making them a part of a missionary task force. In Luke 8 we find what has been called the "first and most amazing evangelistic team ever assembled in the history of Christian mission" (Mortimer Arias, cited in Sider: 66):

Soon afterwards [Jesus] went on through cities and villages, proclaiming and bringing the good news of the kingdom of God. The twelve were with him, as well as some women who had been cured of evil spir-

its and infirmities: Mary, called Magdalene, from
whom seven demons had gone out, and Joanna, the
wife of Herod's steward Chuza, and Susanna, and
many others, who provided for them out of their resources (8:1-3).

Luke dignifies woman's traditional role by having
them supply and prepare food for the needy. He urges the
disciples to do the same (22:26-27), which they are fulfilling in Acts 6:1-6. At the end of his Gospel, Luke records
women as special witnesses to the crucifixion and burial
along with other disciples (23:28-31, 49). But women are
also the first witnesses to the resurrection. They become
the first to proclaim the good news of the resurrection
(24:1-12).

The special role of women continues in Acts. After list-
ing the eleven disciples waiting in the room upstairs, Luke
adds, "All these were constantly devoting themselves to
prayer, together with certain women, including Mary the
mother of Jesus, as well as his brothers" (Acts 1:14).

We noted earlier that Luke emphasizes the role of
women as prophets and persons empowered to speak for
God. This is further demonstrated in Peter's speech on the
day of Pentecost; women are specifically included as
prophesying, shown by the added italics:

> In the last days it will be, God declares,
>   that I will pour out my Spirit upon all flesh,
>   and your sons and your *daughters* shall prophesy,
>   and your young men shall see visions,
>   and your old men shall dream dreams.
> Even upon my slaves, both men and *women*,
>   in those days I will pour out my Spirit;
>   and they shall prophesy. (Acts 2:17-18, from Joel)

Even in Paul's ministry, women are important and spokespersons for God. In 18:24-26, Priscilla is the chief leader since her name is first in Luke's text. She and her husband, Aquilla, correct the theology of a man (Apollos), who "was an eloquent man, well-versed in the scriptures" (18:24). The prophetic gift is also expressed by the four unmarried daughters of Philip the evangelist, one of the seven (21:8-9). Luke certainly wants to make it clear that there were female prophets in the primitive church. Women were regularly outcasts in society, but Luke shows that they have fully entered the reign of God.

Thus far we have seen that Luke portrays a picture of Christ leading in proclaiming the gospel to the marginalized. Luke shows his followers living out that lifestyle of sensitivity as part of their gospel presentation. Luke's wholistic evangelism affirms, embraces, and gives hope to the weak and lowly:

> The insignificant and oppressed people of Israel: the poor, the bonded slaves, the lepers, the women, the children; the enemies of Israel: Gentiles and Samaritans; those regarded as sell-outs: the toll-collectors; all of those who were accustomed to cringing in the presence of the social and religious establishment, are empowered to lift up their heads and hold them high, to recognize their own dignity, to begin to see themselves in a new light. After their encounter with Jesus, they are transformed into people who know themselves to be God's children. (Bosch, 1989:8)

Challenge

Luke's evangelism, we are arguing, functions in a double way: Hope and Challenge. Thus far we have shown that it brings good news and hope to the marginalized and outcast. It is a message of liberation and redemption. However, it is also a challenge to the powerful and those who reject the call to repentance. On this side, it functions confrontationally. Jesus and his followers' evangelization produced conflict.

The gospel will always produce a negative response from those who question its validity and to many who are challenged by it. Mortimer Arias states that "because the new order of God is a threat to any established order, the arrival of the kingdom, forcing its way through the old order, produces a more intense reaction. It attracts and repels at the same time" (43; cf. Krass: 112).

This aspect of Luke's missiology has been used in the great debate as to whether Jesus was a political revolutionary, and whether God's reign is political. Both David Bosch (1991:33-34) and Emilio Castro (58) say, "Yes, but. . . ." It is not political in the modern sense of party politics. Jesus' ministry must not be directly applied to our contemporary controversies, says Bosch. Jesus did not address the big structures of his time, such as Rome. His immediate concern was the world of Palestine, the Jewish establishment rather than the Roman one.

Jesus was not a Zealot. Yet he was quite political in the sense of forming a contrast community, a new peoplehood, as Bosch maintains:

> To declare lepers, tax-collectors, sinners, and the poor to be 'children of God's kingdom' is a decidedly political statement, at least over against the Jewish establishment of the day. It expresses a profound discontent with the way things are, a fervent desire to see them changed. It doesn't wipe out the oppressive circumstances; but it assures the victims that they are no longer prisoners of an omnipotent fate. (Bosch, 1991:33-34)

Castro goes even further: Jesus' "prophetic and messianic vocation led him to confrontation with the historical forces of oppression and the powers and principalities of his day" (58). If this is political, then Jesus' evangelism was political.

Although Jesus' challenge was directed mostly to human beings, Luke makes it clear that it is not limited to that. His challenge extended to spiritual forces, demonic powers which opposed the reign of God. As shown below, Jesus' healing the sick and expelling demons is part of his assault on forces which hinder persons from entering the reign of God. In the first-century Palestinian world, many people believed that Satan could show that he was ruler of the world through his possession of a person, either mentally or physically. Hence, Jesus' successful challenge of the demons proved that the reign of God had arrived.

However, for the most part, Jesus challenged human attitudes, practices, and structures which oppressed and excluded particular categories of persons. For Luke, in the majority of cases, the rich[13] are the ones who are greedy and oppressing and exploiting the poor.[14] With this challenge, Jesus wants the rich to be reconciled to his way of life, to be motivated to a radical conversion, and to enter into God's reign.

The confrontational nature of God's reign is seen in Luke's Christmas story. In 1:5 we are told that Jesus' birth occurs in the days of King Herod of Judea. In 1:26 the angel who announces the conception is Gabriel, whose name means "God is mighty" or "God's mighty warrior." This leads Brueggemann to suggest that the issue in the narrative is not the virgin birth but the power of Herod versus Gabriel (23). Whether this conclusion has merit or not, even in the Magnificat, Mary highlights this conflict when she sings:

> He has shown his strength with his arm;
>> he has scattered the proud in the thought of their
>> hearts.
> He has brought down the powerful from their
>> thrones,
>> and lifted up the lowly. (Luke 1:51-52)

The theme of confrontation appears also in the story of the shepherds. When the angels give hope to the lowly shepherds, they implicitly challenge the powerful. Then the temple scene is explicit. Simeon's words at the dedication of Jesus illustrate the conflictive nature of Jesus' vocation. After Simeon blessed the baby, he said to his mother, Mary: "This child is destined for the falling and the rising of many in Israel, and to be a sign that will be opposed so that the inner thoughts of many will be revealed—and a sword will pierce your own soul too" (Luke 2:34-35).

The evangelism of John the Baptist illustrates the piercing nature of the task. John not only calls for repentance but proclaims the imminent wrath of God:

> John said to the crowds that came to be baptized by him, "You brood of vipers! Who warned you to flee from the wrath to come? Bear fruits worthy of repentance. . . . Even now the ax is lying at the root of the trees; every tree therefore that does not bear good fruit is cut down and thrown into the fire. (Luke 3:7-9)

John's words seem harsh in light of the fact that the crowds have come for baptism. Even the social demands which follow are not friendly, status-quo requirements. Yet Luke is quite intentional in including this narrative, to demonstrate that the call to enter the reign of God has challenges and unconventional demands.

Not until chapter 6 does Luke have Jesus in a confrontational mode with the economically powerful. In 6:20-24 he blesses the poor and pronounces woes on the rich. Jesus' challenge to the rich is part of the good news to the poor. But the woes are balanced with the call and the challenge to share. However, if the rich fail to share, the great reversal spoken of here and earlier in Mary's Magnificat will certainly be realized; all they can expect are woes.

Not until chapter 12 does Luke intensify his criticism of the rich. Yet here and there, this issue weaves its way into parables, stories, and injunctions. One such is the parable of the sower, in which Jesus speaks adversely of the rich. In 8:14 he makes reference to those who are choked by the cares, riches, and pleasures of life. Thus the parable indirectly supports the position of Jesus in Luke that the life of the rich is not a positive one (Cassidy: 28).

In Luke 12:13-34, Jesus speaks out against the abundance of possessions of the rich and challenges the disciples not to worry about material possessions. The discourse begins with someone in the crowd asking Jesus' help in obtaining a share of an inheritance. Jesus takes the opportunity to declare that a person's life does not consist in the abundance of possessions. He then tells the parable of the rich fool (12:16-21), which focuses on the accumulation of goods.[15] For holding onto so many possessions and refusing to share, he is declared a fool. God tells him that his life will be required of him that very night.

Then Jesus declares, "So it is with those who store up treasures for themselves but are not rich toward God" (Luke 12:21). In this context, we must understand Jesus' immediate challenge to his disciples not to worry about their life, what they will eat, or their body, what they will wear (12:22). Instead, they should sell their possessions and give alms (12:33).

The other parable which challenges the lack of sharing one's bounty is that of the rich man and Lazarus (16:19-

31). In this parable, as in the one about the rich fool (12:16-21), Luke does not focus on how they obtained their riches, or even on whether they exploited their workers to obtain such large possessions (Maynard-Reid, 1990:67). It would be assumed by his readers that all rich persons have obtained their riches through oppressive means. Yet Jesus' overriding concern in these parables is what the rich people did or didn't do with their great possessions.

The rich fool of chapter 12 thinks only of himself without any concern for others. The rich man of chapter 16 has no concern at all for the poor man Lazarus who sat at his gate. Both these wealthy persons are condemned because they have failed to share their abundance with those who lack even basic necessities. They think only of themselves. The rich fail to accept the social challenge which Luke has John the Baptist giving as a requirement to enter the reign of God (3:10-14). By rejecting opportunities to share, they bring upon themselves the loss of life (12:20) and the torments of Hades (16:23).

I have noted elsewhere that there is another subtle area of condemnation particularly in the story of the rich man and Lazarus (Maynard-Reid, 1990:67). In addition to the condemnation for not sharing, there is an implicit critique of the luxurious living of the rich. This extravagance is exposed and apparently denounced in the detailed description of the rich man "dressed in purple and fine linen," who "feasted sumptuously" (16:19).

Since the parable of the rich fool (Luke 12:16-21) is directly followed by the sayings on worry (12:22-34), this also seems to confirm a condemnation of a sumptuous lifestyle. Here Jesus tells his disciples not to worry about what they eat or what they wear (12:22). Then he uses the parable of the rich to challenge the disciples against concern for luxurious living: "Consider the lilies, how they grow: they neither toil or spin; yet I tell you, even Solomon in all his glory was not clothed like one of these. But if God so clothes the grass of the field, which is alive today and tomorrow is thrown in the oven, how much more will he clothe you—you of little faith!" (12:27-28).

As in the parable of the rich man and Lazarus, Jesus parallels the clothing with the eating. "Do not keep striving for what you are to eat and what you are to drink, and do not keep worrying. For it is the nations of the world that strive after all these things, and your Father knows that you need them" (Luke 12:29-30). Hence, luxurious living which consumes one's entire life and the failure to share with the needy are both presented as lifestyles which cut one off from the reign of God. Instead, they make one a candidate for damnation.

An even more forceful incident illustrates the socially confrontational nature of the call to enter the reign of God. This is found in Luke's presentation of Jesus' dialogue with the rich ruler and the follow-up dialogue with his disciples (Luke 18:18-30). Like the crowds asking John the Baptist what they should do (3:10-14), the ruler asks Jesus, "What must I do to inherit eternal life?" (18:18). Jesus' response is just as stunning as was John the Baptist's. "There is still one thing lacking. Sell all that you own and distribute the money to the poor, and you will have treasure in heaven; then come, follow me" (18:22).

The ruler rejected Jesus' challenge and turned away sad. This attitude elicited Jesus' famous reaction: "How hard it is for those who have wealth to enter the kingdom of God! Indeed, it is easier for a camel to go through the eye of a needle than for someone who is rich to enter the kingdom of God" (18:24-25). This logion of Jesus has been totally misinterpreted:

> We need to read this narrative literally and as rigor-
> ously as Jesus intended his words to be understood. It

> is a pity that Christian interpreters a century or so
> later—not coming to grips with the stringency of the
> saying, and anxious to conciliate the wealthy who
> were joining the church—invented the meaning of
> "rope" for the Greek word "camel" or also suggested
> that the "eye of the needle" was a small gate in Jerusa-
> lem through which a camel could pass only on its
> knees. (Maynard-Reid, 1990:68; cf. 1987:34-35)

In this passage as in the teaching about the rich fool, Jesus is saying that if the wealthy of his day intend to enter God's reign, they have to give up their wealth which they have gained selfishly and oppressively. They must share possessions with the less fortunate to fulfill in part their hope of sharing in the riches of the reign of God.

In contrast to Matthew and Mark, Jesus' words in Luke about the difficulty of the rich entering the reign of God are not addressed to the disciples. They have already accepted the challenge and made themselves poor in becoming disciples.[16] Instead, the challenge is directly and totally addressed to the wealthy ruler. This ruler can't receive eternal life because he rejects Jesus' call. But the disciples have the firm promise of eternal life (18:29-30). The woes fall upon the ruler, the blessings on the disciples—an illustration and fulfillment of 6:20-26 (Tannehill, 1986:122).

We cannot overstress the role of *sharing* in Luke's missiology. Challenging the rich to share is part of the good news to the poor. "The coming of God's reign can . . . be good news for the poor if it transforms people of prosperity so that they share with the poor. This is an important goal of Jesus' teaching in Luke" (Tannehill, 1986:129).

This emphasis on sharing comes out clearly when we notice how Luke treats Jesus' sayings in the Sermon on the Level Place (Luke) or Mount (Matthew). The focus in Luke is definitely on the conduct of the rich to the poor. Thus when Matthew (5:44) records "love your enemies," Luke (6:27) parallels that but redefines enemies as those who don't repay their debts! (6:35). The passages in parallel columns show the differences through added italics:

Matthew 5:42-48	Luke 6:30-36
Give to everyone who begs from you, and do not refuse anyone who wants to borrow from you.	Give to everyone who begs from you; and if anyone takes away your goods, do not ask for them again. Do to others as you would have them do to you.
You have heard that it was said, "You shall love your neighbor and hate your enemy." But I say to you, *Love your enemies and pray for those who persecute you*, so that you may be children of your Father in heaven; for he makes his sun to rise on the evil and on the good, and sends rain on the righteous and on the unrighteous. For if you love those who love you, what reward do you have? Do not even the tax collectors do the same? And if you greet only your brother and sisters, what more are you doing than others? Do not even the Gentiles do the same? *Be perfect*, therefore, as your heavenly Father is perfect.	If you love those who love you, what credit is that to you? For even sinners love those who love them. If you do good to those who do good to you, what credit is that to you? For even sinners do the same. If you lend to those from whom you hope to receive, what credit is that to you? Even sinners lend to sinners, to receive as much again. *But love your enemies, do good, and lend, expecting nothing in return.* Your reward will be great, and you will be children of the Most High; for he is kind to the ungrateful and the wicked. *Be merciful*, just as your Father is merciful.

This challenge to show mercy and demonstrate love through sharing, "expecting nothing in return," is a prerequisite to entering the reign of God. Similarly, after Jesus tells the parable of the great dinner (Luke 14:15-24), giving hope to the outcast, poor, and marginal, he emphasizes what it takes to follow him as a disciple (14:35-35). He gives a radical call to discipleship and ends with the statement, "So therefore, none of you can become my disciple if you do not give up all your possessions" (14:33).

Jesus' disciples have fulfilled that entrance requirement for the reign of God. Immediately after the dialogue with the rich ruler (Luke 18:18-27), Peter says to Jesus, "Look, we have left our homes and followed you." In response, Jesus praises those who give up possessions: "Truly I tell you, there is no one who has left house or wife or brothers or parents or children, for the sake of the kingdom of God, who will not get back very much more in this age, and in the age to come eternal life" (18:28-30).

Zacchaeus is the classic case of one who responds to Jesus' challenge and confrontation of his rich and oppressive lifestyle (Luke 19:1-10). It is placed in close proximity to the narrative of the rich ruler and thus provides a living example of how a rich person can be saved. Jim Wallis is on target: the significance of the Zacchaeus story "is not that Zacchaeus was so short he had to climb a tree to see Jesus, as children are often taught in their Sunday school lessons." Instead, the focus is on Zacchaeus "repenting of sin and turning to Jesus [and this involved] *making reparation to the poor*" (1976:27).

This narrative is the best example in the Gospel of those who have embraced Jesus' teaching. It shows that the proper response to the reign of God involves a reorientation of our values in line with those of the kingdom (Dyrness: 136). The values called for by Jesus and demonstrated in the salvation of Zacchaeus involve the conversion of greed into generosity, dishonest dealings into restitution (Posterski: 24). There was a behavioral change which required an end to his oppression of the poor and a sharing of his ill-gotten wealth.

Luke then presents the primitive church as a concrete example of persons who have renounced their possessions to follow the Christian Way. The emphasis placed on this, especially in the two summaries in Acts 2:42-47 and 4:32-37, demonstrates forcefully that Luke's concern for the poor and his challenge to the rich does not disappear at all in Acts (Tannehill, 1990:46). The sharing in the Jerusalem church represents a wholehearted obedience to Jesus' teaching regarding possessions in Luke.

Thus in Luke 18:22, Luke has Jesus telling the rich ruler to "sell" and "distribute" to the poor. These two words occur in a significant passage of Acts, showing fulfillment of Jesus' command (italics added):

> Now the whole group of those who believed were of one heart and soul, and no one claimed private ownership of any possessions, but everything they owned was held in common. . . . There was not a needy person among them, for as many as owned lands or houses *sold* them and brought the proceeds of what was sold. They laid it at the apostles' feet, and it was *distributed* to each as any had need. (4:32-35)[17]

For Luke's theological and missionary purposes, it was just as vital for him to locate this scene early in Acts, as it was for him to place Mary's song early in his Gospel. It shows the believers' reaction to the Pentecost experience and the result of Pentecost. Both stories have a social content in the account of a new age beginning. As William Dyrness maintains, the Pentecost experience in Acts is put in obvious parallel with the birth narrative. In both, the power of salvation is entering the world. "As a response to the coming of the Holy Spirit and in fulfillment of Mary's song in Luke 1:53, the believers sold all their possessions and distributed to any that had need" (155-156).

One oft-ignored incident illustrates the lifestyle Jesus demanded. In the narration of Peter healing the lame beggar at the gate of the temple called Beautiful, he declares to the lame man, "I have no silver or gold" (Acts 3:1-10). This implies that Peter has renounced his possessions along with the rest of the primitive Christian community (2:44-45). Earlier he had left all to follow Jesus (Luke 5:11; 18:28).

There is clearly a trajectory going through Luke-Acts which demonstrates that part of the evangelistic task is to challenge the rich and powerful to give up their possessions and share them with those in need. The same challenge is also given to any who seek to become Jesus' disciples and enter the reign of God. By modeling this lifestyle, the primitive church was living out its evangelistic task. Their evangelism, then, says Escobar, was not only by a way of speaking but by a way of being. They were messengers by word and deed (308).

Acts, Luke's second volume, does not portray the primitive church in as direct and explicit confrontation with socioeconomic powers and persons as was Jesus in Gospel of Luke. Yet the apostles are still shown to be in serious conflict as they are involved in their evangelistic enterprise. They were regularly at odds with the authorities. David Bosch states that their mission was political, revolutionary, and subversive (1991:47).

It was revolutionary to confess Jesus as Lord. The new relationships were revolutionary: Jew and Roman, Greek and barbarian, free and slave, rich and poor, woman and man—all were accepted as brothers and sisters. "Small wonder that the early Christian community caused so much astonishment in the Roman Empire and beyond. . . . What Christians were and did simply fell outside of the frame of reference of many philosophies of that period" (Bosch, 1991:48). It was truly a contrast community.

According to Acts, apostles like Peter, James, and John were challenging the Jewish authorities and consistently in mortal danger from them (4:1-22; 5:17-42; 8:1-3; 12:1-19). Others in the community, like Stephen in his proclamation and practice of the gospel (6:8—8:3), showed how believers were in conflict with the forces of evil. In Paul's missionary journeys, his evangelistic practices challenged all aspects of evil—spiritual, social, economic, and political.

In Philippi, the spiritual liberation of a girl who had a spirit of divination affected the social and financial life of her owners, who made much money from her fortune-telling. They in turn brought political accusations against Paul and Silas, who were summarily thrown into prison and charged with "disturbing the city" and advocating customs not lawful for Romans to adopt (Acts 16:16-40).

A similar situation occurred in Ephesus, where the end of idolatry jolted the business structure of the major city in Asia Minor, causing a riot (19:21-41; Escobar: 309). Such a challenge to any existing order demonstrates that the reign of God, according to Arias, is "an irreverent exposure of human motivations and of the most sacred rules of human mores." This reign "is an iconoclastic disturber of religious sacred places and customs and the most radical threat to temple, altars, priestly castes, and the most protected 'holiest of holies' " (Arias: 47).

The evangelistic enterprise, then, as delineated by Luke-Acts, not only brings hope to the marginal and outcast, spiritually and socially. It also challenges the forces which war against the reign of God and assures them of destruction. True evangelism holds out the invitation for the rich to accept the gospel invitation and share in God's reign by relinquishing their earthly social power.

4

Theological Motifs in Luke-Acts

The biblical authors and particularly the Gospel writers were not systematic theologians in our modern Western sense of the discipline. They were storytellers who used narrative to communicate their theology, a theology which grew out of their missionary enterprise. It would therefore be wrongheaded for us to think we can gain the essence of Luke's theological and missiological worldview by reducing his work into small systematic categories.

Hence, taking a trajectory through the two-volume work is more helpful than systematizing Luke's message. Telling the story again can be more rewarding than attempting to analyze through artificially created categories.

At the same time, the history of Western theological reflection has created certain categories which have helped us gain a handle on the biblical thought world. Inadequate as it may be, and limited as it has been found—particularly by theologians from the two-thirds world and other marginal groups in the Northern and Western world—we can gain insights into Luke's evangelistic program by summarizing these foci.

In Luke-Acts certain themes appear again and again: the reign of God, salvation, repentance, conversion, the role of the Holy Spirit. These themes are not rigidly separate; they interrelate and are interwoven with one another. In the same way, other categories, many times left out in traditional theological discussions, interrelate with themselves and with these. For example, such issues as poverty and wealth, oppression, justice and fairness in human relationships—these consistently occur in connection with the previously stated themes. Yet at the root of Luke's theology and missiology is the overriding theme of the reign of God and one's entrance into that reign.

The Reign of God

In recent decades much has been written on the reign of God (or the kingdom of God, as it has traditionally been translated). George Eldon Ladd (118-144) has summarized the extensive debate on whether the "kingdom of God" concept is reign or realm, eschatological or non-eschatological, localized or timeless. Other discussions center around whether it is spiritual or social, religious or political.

Leonardo Bott, in his *New Evangelization*, notes that

the figure of the reign is a holistic, political category. Biblically it signifies the totality of creation redeemed and organized on the criteria of God's loving design. The reign represents the comprehensive politics of God, to be implemented in the history of the cosmos, of nations, of the chosen people, and in the depths of each human heart. In the Western inculturation the reign was transformed into a synonym for the other world, the afterlife. It suffered a profound spiritualization, a complete depoliticization. (32)

Some may be uncomfortable with neo-politicization of the concept *reign,* because of contemporary usage of the term (with negative baggage). Yet even if we contend that it is spiritual, we must recapture the meaning of the concept *spiritual,* with its wholism—social, religious, and even political (in its positive sense of peoplehood), in which God is central.

The concept of the reign of God is comprehensive and fluid. Donald Senior sees it in Judaism as three-dimensional. First, it has an eschatological character. It deals with the ultimate destiny of Israel. Second, it has a theological character. It denotes the coming rule of God—God's very presence among them. And third, it has a soteriological or saving character. God who comes will save his people from pain, sickness, evil, and death (145; cf. Castro: 48).

In Jesus' ministry, it is just as comprehensive and fluid, multidimensional and all-encompassing. It includes the inner life of the individual. But to limit God's reign to that is totally inadequate. It extends beyond the individual soul to the whole of society. "It embraces all dimensions of human life: physical, spiritual, personal, and interpersonal, communal and societal, historical and eternal. And it encompasses all human relationship—with the neighbor, with nature, and with God" (Arias: xv; cf. Verkuyl: 197).

The sum total of Jesus' ministry defines the concept of the reign of God. All his activities and his teaching illustrations give substance to an abstract symbol. His parables about God's graciousness, his association with outcasts and women, his healing the sick and expelling demons— all offer us a glimpse of what the kingdom of God means (Senior: 146, 151). If anyone continues the traditional reductionist version of the reign of God in the ministry of Jesus, that does total injustice to Luke's use of the concept in his Gospel.

In Acts, Luke's concern for the reign of God is not lessened. The apostolic preaching is about this reign. The dialogue with Jesus and his disciples at the beginning of the second volume (Acts 1) demonstrates that to be a witness of Jesus means that one is a witness to the reign of God (cf. Luke 24:48). To announce Jesus is to announce the reign of God. They are synonymous.

Luke specifically points to Philip in Samaria proclaiming the good news about the reign of God (Acts 8:12). And Luke is careful to demonstrate that in the missionary journeys of Paul, this focus is still central—at Antioch (14:22), at Ephesus (19:8), and in Rome, as he brings his two-volume work to a close (28:23, 30-31; Arias: 59-60).

Some interpreters are trying to help us see the reign of God as the Eastern mind (the biblical writers) would see it, as a dynamic rule rather than a spatial realm (Dyrness: 126). Yet the debate continues as to the temporal and spatial nature of the reign.

Jesus' sayings about the timing, timetable, and place of God's reign seem to be inconsistent. Some statements appear to indicate that it is present and now, while others point to the future, after some significant interval. One may conclude that there is ambiguity and contradiction in the teaching of Jesus and the early church on the reign of God.

For centuries there has been no question as to the future nature of Christ's reign. Luke's Gospel, and Acts as well, places it in an eschatological future. A series of parousia parables in the Gospel speaks to this. The parables of the doorkeeper (Luke 12:35-38), the nocturnal burglar (12:39-40), the faithful and prudent manager (12:41-46), and the ten pounds (19:11-27)—all seem to indicate that for Jesus the coming reign of God is still future.

The classic apocalyptic discourse of Luke 21 makes it clear that the reign of God is definitely not present, at least not in fullness. After using typical apocalyptic language to describe what will happen at the end of this earth's existence (signs in the sun, moon, and stars, etc.), Jesus says, "So also, when you see these things taking place, you know that the kingdom of God is near" (21:31).

Jesus follows this up by stating that "this generation will not pass away until all things have taken place" (Luke 21:32). Thus he seems to indicate that fulfillment is in the near future. Yet the passage has been interpreted by generation after generation to be referring to each reader's generation, putting it further into the future. However the text is read, it is difficult to ignore the fact that in these passages, the reign of God is later than when Jesus is uttering these sayings.

This position seems to be affirmed by the final dialogue with Jesus and his disciples. They are still seeking an earthly and present kingdom. His reply dispels that:

> So when they had come together, they asked him, "Lord, is this the time when you will restore the kingdom to Israel?" He replied, "It is not for you to know the times or periods that the Father has set by his own authority. But you will receive power when the Holy Spirit has come upon you; and you will be my witnesses in Jerusalem, in all Judea and Samaria, and to the ends of the earth. (Acts 1:6-8)

The disciples are thinking of the restoration of the literal Davidic kingdom. But Jesus has been trying to move their minds away to a broader scope and a future dimension for the reign-of-God concept.

Many interpreters also maintain that the reign of God was present in Jesus' Palestinian ministry. G. V. Pixley (64-87), for example, argues that the reign that Jesus announced and was inaugurating in the first century was really a political prospect of justice and freedom for the working people of Palestine, especially Galilee.

We may not want to go as far as Pixley; yet it does seem that Luke witnesses to the reality that the reign of God has arrived in Jesus' life and ministry. In Jesus' strident response to those accusing him of casting out demons by Beelzebul, he says, "Now if I cast out the demons by Beelzebul, by whom do your exorcists cast them out? . . . But if it is by the finger of God that I cast out the demons, then the kingdom of God has come to you" (Luke 11:19-20).

The most cogent passage regarding the presence of the kingdom is found in Luke 17:20-21. Here one of the Pharisees asks Jesus when the reign of God will arrive. Jesus responds, "The kingdom of God is not coming with things that can be observed; nor will they say, 'Look, here it is!' or 'There it is!' For, in fact, the kingdom of God is among you." Although there remains some objection,[1] most New Testament scholars are agreed that Jesus here intended to argue that in him the reign of God was presently being realized.

Finally, just as there are parousia parables in Luke, there are also presence parables. Parables such as the sower (8:5-8) and the mustard seed (13:18-19) and the yeast (13:20-21) all seem to emphasize that the reign of God is a present reality and has already dawned.

In Luke, the reign of God is both future and present. Luke is actually working with the apocalyptic idea that the future has invaded the present, while it is still yet to come in fullness. The "not yet" has already begun. Both the "already" and the "not yet" aspects of the reign of God are part of the essence of Jesus' person and ministry. Although the hour of darkness—sin, suffering, and death—still exist, the reign of God is a light breaking through and impinging on the present. Yet there is still the looking forward to the full and bright revelation.

Luke's Gospel (like the other three) is a theological interpretation of Jesus' life and ministry. It was created and edited under the inspiration of the Holy Spirit to address contemporary issues many years after Jesus' resurrection and ascension, and to express the self-definition of Luke's audience. Luke, therefore, sees the reign-of-God concept as important in the life and theology of his community. It is not simply a historic idea limited to the pre-resurrection ministry of Jesus. Luke sets it out as a paradigm for the universal church fifty years after the Easter event.

Therefore, I conclude that what the dynamic reign of God was for Jesus, Luke's community, and his theology, it should also be for us: future and present, "already" and "not yet." I agree with Donald Senior that the kingdom of God is not reducible to a moment in history or some localized set of events and circumstances. It is "an experience of God's rule; it is a metaphor describing a *quality* of life and not just a reference to the climax (or termination) of history" (155). Present experiences are part of the reign of God. Yet the cosmic consummation is future (155).

For Luke, the personal and social evangelistic mission of both Jesus and the early church had reference to the initiation of believers into that reign now, while at the same time they were awaiting the final glorious eschatological reign of God.

Salvation

Luke, more than any other New Testament writer, underscores extensively the fact that salvation is not simply a private relationship between God and the individual. Yes, it is interpersonal; but it is so both vertically and horizontally. Both God and one's fellow human beings are involved. If the reign of God impinges on the entire present, then salvation cannot be limited to the individual soul.

Sine rightly notes that if the reign of God has not only

come to transform us but the world, "then clearly we are a part of something much larger than just our own personal salvation" (Sine: 25). Likewise, Jim Wallis lists this as part of an *Agenda for a Biblical People:*

> Salvation must not be seen as merely an individual event in which the individual has a part. The kingdom of God has come to transform the world and us with it by the power of God in Jesus Christ. The cross of Christ is not just the symbol of our atonement but the very pattern and definition of our lives, the very means of the new order that has invaded the world in Christ. (1976:30)

Yet when we think of salvation in relation to the cross and atonement, we normally arrive at an individualistic and largely forensic notion of justification. For this we have to thank Luther's misunderstanding of a Pauline concept. In reality, Paul's idea of justification and salvation, rather than being forensically understood by his audience (or intended by him), was closer to the Synoptic idea of the reign of God. The early church understood the concept dynamically. But it evolved into a "dehistoricized, individual, salvation-or-damnation eschatology" (Krass: 29; cf. Sider: 82, 88).

It is sad that when one consults a standard theological dictionary for the term *salvation*, the definition and categories include justification, reconciliation, propitiation, adoption, redemption, new birth, etc. But categories which include the social, economic, political, and physical are missing (Pannell: 26, 36).

There is no single understanding of Christ's saving work or one metaphor that says it all. The work of Luke demonstrates a varied understanding of the concept. He integrates various interrelated aspects of salvation (Sider:

87, 94ff.), with Christ at the center of all. For Luke, salvation is not an abstract idea limited to either one or another dimension. It is an end to all death and injustice. It includes all transforming acts. Any action taken to effect a reversal of evil—spiritual, social, economic, political, physical, and psychological—was salvific. All of human life could and should be transformed under the impact of Christ and of his followers' ministry, according to Luke.

Of the many dimensions of salvation, Luke gives more special attention to the social than any other New Testament author. A primary understanding of salvation for him is the exaltation and redemption of marginal persons. He bestows dignity upon them. Luke has Jesus and his followers intervening on the side of the oppressed and excluded, assuring them that they share in God's salvation.

These groups include the poor, sinners, tax collectors, women, Samaritans, and foreigners—groups excluded or subordinated in first-century Palestine. Luke shows that the Jesus Movement had a special interest in ministering to such people (Tannehill, 1986:103; Bosch, 1989:8).

This social dimension of salvation is presented early in the Gospel. The entire Magnificat of Mary (Luke 1:46-55) is rooted in the salvation motif. And the social reversal theme in 1:51-53 is certainly included in this salvific theme—the hungry filled, the rich turned away empty.

Yet the Benedictus of Zechariah (Luke 1:67-79) is the most explicit. Some see it as giving a clear statement of political salvation:

> He has raised up a mighty savior for us
> in the house of his servant David,
> as he spoke through the mouth of his holy prophets
> from of old,
> that we would be saved from our enemies and from
> the hand of all who hate us. (1:69-71)

To suppose that Luke could not be thinking in such political terms is to ignore the tragic line of the story, according to Tannehill. "The story is presenting a real possibility and a valid hope which was tragically rejected at the moment of fulfillment" (1986:26). Israel was hoping to become an independent state with their own king, but thus far was disappointed (1986:26). This was the salvation Zechariah sings about.

However, Zechariah later states that the child is called "to give knowledge of salvation to his people by the forgiveness of their sins" (1:77). Therefore, we have to perceive that Zechariah's thoughts go beyond the political to a wider dimension.

The theme continues in Luke 2 with the angels giving "glory to God in the highest heaven" (2:14). The lowly shepherds (low among social classes of the time) were directly told that "to *you* is born this day in the city of David a Savior, who is the Messiah, the Lord" (2:11, italics added). This must have led them to understand "the savior" in social terms. So if we recognize that Luke wants to stress this social aspect, there is no reason why we should attempt to interpret the annunciation without this dimension.

The Nunc Dimittis (Luke 2:29-32) of Simeon also focuses on salvation. This old man, "looking forward to the consolation of Israel" (2:25), rejoices to see the baby:

> My eyes have seen your salvation,
> which you have prepared in the presence of all peoples,
> a light for revelation to the Gentiles
> and for glory to your people Israel. (2:30-32)

Here Simeon is expanding the messianic hope to even the despised foreigners!

The narrative of the proclamation of John the Baptist

(3:1-18) is different from accounts in the other Gospels. Luke's presentation is unique in its social challenge and in its demands on the hearers. Luke alone clearly has a salvation emphasis in this narrative. We will follow Rice (100-101) and set up some parallels to show Luke's unique focus on the role of John the Baptist.

MATTHEW	MARK	LUKE
The voice of one crying out in the wilderness: "Prepare the way of the Lord, make his path straight" (3:4).	See, I am sending my messenger ahead of you, who will prepare your way; the voice of one crying out in the wilderness: "Prepare the way of the Lord, make his paths straight" (1:2-3).	The voice of one crying out in the wilderness: "Prepare the way of the Lord, make his paths straight. Every valley shall be filled, and every mountain and hill shall be made low, and the crooked shall be made straight, and the rough ways made smooth; and all flesh shall see the salvation of God (3:4-6).

All three authors quote from Isaiah 40:3-5, but only Luke has an extensive quotation with a reversal theme in line with his social-reversal focus. Luke even adapts the last phrase of Isaiah to demonstrate the salvation aspect which John is announcing:

ISAIAH 40:5	LUKE 3:6
Then the glory of the Lord shall be revealed, and all people shall see it together, for the mouth of the Lord has spoken.	And all flesh shall see the salvation of God.

Luke wishes to emphasize the theme of salvation in the same context that he presents John the Baptist's unique social proclamation. While the other Evangelists emphasize John the Baptist as a forerunner, Luke has him as an announcer of a special dimension of salvation.

The social dimension of salvation is even more forceful in the rich ruler narrative (Luke 18:18-30). First, when the ruler inquires how eternal life is secured, Jesus recites parts of the Ten Commandments which relate people with people, not the ones which relate people with God (Luke 18:20, as in Mark; Pannell: 35). Second, after Jesus announces the impossibility for a rich person to enter the reign of God, those who hear it say, "Then who can be saved?" (18:26). Jesus' reply means that salvation comes to those willing to give up "all" (18:22, 29) their possessions and share with those who lack basic necessities.

The story of Zacchaeus (19:1-10) is placed near the story of the rich ruler to show how a rich person can receive salvation in the present. Zacchaeus's announcement of economic reparation elicited these words from Jesus: "Today salvation has come to this house" (19:9). In this context, David Bosch points out that salvation in Luke involves a reversal of the evil consequences of sin both horizontally and vertically. Both God and neighbor are involved.

"Zacchaeus is not only inwardly liberated from all the ties of his possessions, but actually does reparation." Bosch further emphasizes that "liberation *from* is also liberation *to*, else it is not an expression of salvation" (1991:107). Salvation is weighed in the balance and found wanting if this social aspect is not included—at least as far as Luke is concerned.

Luke's understanding of salvation goes beyond the socioeconomic and includes his healing activities, which is certainly a dimension of social salvation. This ministry "demonstrated that the saving grace of God extends not only to personal guilt and broken relationships but to human bodies, to societal structures, to mysterious forces that hold creation itself in check" (Senior: 151).

This fact is emphasized by Luke's use of the term *sōzein*, "to save." The evangelist used it to describe what Jesus did in face of sickness, demon possession, and exploitation. It was not an exclusively "religious" term, as often used in contemporary religious circles. In Luke, it is also used for healing. There is "no tension between saving from sin and saving from physical ailment, between spiritual and social" (Bosch, 1991:33).

The healing narratives show that there is a strong connection between all aspects of God's redemptive purpose and the healing activities. For Luke, the healing work of Jesus is part of the larger saving purpose of God for the world. That purpose embraces the physical as well as other dimensions of life (Tannehill, 1986:88; cf. Bosch, 1989:11).

When this is grasped, it becomes clearer why Jesus includes "recovery of sight to the blind" (a type of physical problem that stands for all) in his mission statement in Nazareth (Luke 4:18). Jesus recognizes that his mission is to physically save especially the chronically ill—the lepers, blind, deaf, cripples—who were discriminated against, both socially and religiously, in first-century Palestine.

John's Gospel implies it is a widespread belief that their condition was brought on either by their sin or by the sin of their parents (John 9:2). Jesus not only goes against the norms of the religious leaders in Jerusalem, but against the accepted regulations of the conservative Qumran community. The rule of Qumran was that no mad person, lunatic, simpleton or fool, blind person or maiden, lame or deaf person, or minor could enter the community (Arias: 22).[2] On the contrary, these were precisely the ones Jesus saw as candidates for entrance into the reign of God.

Luke closely connects the reign of God and the healing activity. In Luke 9:2, the twelve are given a wholistic commission to proclaim the reign of God and to heal. Then Luke reports that "they departed and went through the villages, bringing the good news and curing diseases everywhere" (9:6). When they returned, Jesus continued to welcome the crowds "and spoke to them about the kingdom of God, and healed those who needed to be cured" (9:11). Placing these in parallel certainly suggests that Luke saw them together as central to the evangelistic task of Jesus and his disciples.

Jesus' commission to the Seventy provides conclusive evidence that Luke connects healing and the reign of God. In 10:1-24 Jesus sends out the Seventy in pairs on an evangelistic mission: "The harvest is plentiful, but the laborers are few; therefore ask the Lord of the harvest to send out laborers into his harvest" (10:2). Jesus' instruction included a significant command: "Cure the sick . . . and say to them, 'The kingdom of God has come near to you' " (10:9). We believe the latter phrase should interpret the former. In their healing, the reign of God has arrived.

A good case which illustrates the interrelatedness of healing and salvation is found in the narrative of the cleansing of the ten lepers (17:11-19). The ten were pleading for Jesus to have mercy upon them. He tells them to go and show themselves to the priests. On their way there, they are healed. The Samaritan among them, when he recognized that he was healed, returns to thank Jesus. Jesus responds, "Get up and go on your way; your faith has made you well" (17:19).

We should not, like Rice, argue that the term *sōzein*, "made well," should be translated "saved" in a spiritual sense in the ten-leper account (105). To do that is to miss the wholistic dimension of salvation in Luke. Luke uses this word to link healing with entrance into the reign of God. It does go beyond physical wellness. The other nine were only healed—the text doesn't say they were saved (an argument from silence, we admit). But this Samaritan's healing involved both the physical and a deeper change, one which produced praise and thanksgiving. He gained comprehensive wholeness.

In Acts, Luke shows that salvation is not limited to the personal, internal, spiritual realm. It is not simply an abstract idea. It includes transforming actions on the part of the followers of the Way. Healing, deliverance, and dramatic social change accompany the apostles' proclamation of the good news about Jesus (Acts 17:6; 19:8-41).

A classic example is the healing of the crippled beggar at the Beautiful Gate (3:1-10). He asks for money, but Peter says that he has no silver or gold. But what he has, he gives him: "In the name of Jesus Christ of Nazareth, stand up and walk" (3:6). He gives him physical salvation. Luke is not attempting to contrast the giving of money and the giving of salvation through Christ. What he does give the lame man is just as social as improving his economic well-being. Physical salvation is what this cripple needs more than anything else. "The lame man becomes a paradigm of salvation through the name of the Lord" (Tannehill, 1990:49). Physical well-being is only salvific if it is in the name of the Lord.[3]

Like healings, casting out unclean spirits has salvific meaning in Luke's work. Jesus performs these under the auspices of the coming, present, and eschatological reign of God. "The overthrow of Satan and the definitive defeat of evil and death were characteristic themes of Jewish apocalyptic" (Senior: 150). Jesus' evangelistic mission had to include liberating people from the grip of evil spirits.

In this context, we can understand the second line in Jesus' evangelistic manifesto. In part, the release of the captives has to do with liberation from demonic possession.[4] Thus the first set of miracles after the Nazareth announcement has to do with demonic possessions. It is probable that Luke purposely placed them next to the Nazareth narrative to demonstrate the working out of Jesus' claim. Without doubt, the healing of the demoniac in the synagogue in Capernaum is a demonstration that Jesus is bringing release and salvation to the captives of Satan (Luke 4:31-37; Rice: 47).

Immediately after this account, we find Jesus with Simeon's mother-in-law, who is sick with a high fever. Jesus "rebuked the fever, and it left her" (Luke 4:39). It is as if the fever had intelligence! So it was thought to have. In the first century, there was widespread belief that various mental and physical disorders were caused by demon possession (Rice: 47; Tannehill, 1986:65) Thus they think the fever demon caused this woman's high fever. In healing her, Jesus releases her from demonic captivity and brings her salvation.

Luke (following Mark) ties healing together with expelling demons in his report of what happens when the Sabbath is over. "As the sun was setting, all those who had any who were sick with various kinds of diseases brought them to him; and he laid his hands on each of them and cured them. Demons also *came out of many*, shouting, 'You are the Son of God!' But he rebuked them and would not allow them to speak, because they knew that he was the Messiah" (Luke 4:40-41).

In the mission of the Seventy, we also find this relation between healing and expelling demons. Jesus tells these evangelists to "cure the sick . . . and say to them, 'The kingdom of God has come near to you' " (Luke 10:9). When they return, they report to Jesus, "Lord, in your name even the demons submit to us!" (10:17).

Jesus responds, "I watched Satan fall from heaven like

a flash of lightning" (10:18). This is a prophetic acknowl-
edgement of the radical defeat of the forces of evil, present
and future. The evil assault on God's reign is being sub-
dued. Instead of Satan and his forces being able to prove
beyond dispute that he is the lord of the world, Jesus and
his evangelists are demonstrating that the reign of God has
arrived and the pillars of Satan's reign are under assault
(Bosch, 1991:33; Castro: 56). Salvation has come to those
previously captives in the realm of Satan.

Likewise, when Jesus heals the crippled woman on the
Sabbath in the synagogue, he describes her as one whom
"Satan bound for eighteen long years" (13:16). In the heal-
ing, Jesus releases her from bondage.

This working of the gospel (good news) was an inte-
gral part of the primitive church's evangelistic mission. In
Peter's recital of the good news before Cornelius and his
household, he says, "God anointed Jesus of Nazareth with
the Holy Spirit and with power; . . . he went about doing
good and healing all who were oppressed by the devil, for
God was with him" (Acts 10:38). Luke is definitely rein-
forcing what his Gospel reports, that Jesus claims he is
"anointed . . . to proclaim release to the captives" (Luke
4:18). The evangelistic task, then, has to include release
from demonic possession.

Hence, Jesus' healing ministry is larger than simply
curing bodies. "It is a proleptic manifestation of the presence of the reign of God, evidence of God 'visiting' humankind" (Bosch, 1989:10). Luke presents Jesus casting
out demons not to show him as another miracle worker or
exorcist of his day (as in Acts 19:13-16), who commonly
uses oaths. Instead, Jesus expels demons with direct commands and without oaths. He demonstrates God's reign
being inaugurated.

We must not leave the impression that salvation for
Luke is a concept which only involves dimensions of the

social, the political, healing, and deliverance from demons. Instead, salvation is comprehensive and includes a personal response of coming to believe in Jesus Christ. Those who have entered the reign of God through those other dimensions are challenged to follow Jesus and become part of his community. Salvation is whole restoration, applied to the whole person, for the whole world, and to curtail all the Satanic powers opposing God.

The final sentence in Acts 2:47 indicates that day after day the Lord is adding to their numbers those who are being saved. This must be taken in the context of 2:43-44, where the apostles are performing "signs and wonders," and the believers have all things in common—sharing their possessions. Salvation for Luke is wholistic. It is the transformation of body, soul, and spirit.

Repentance

Repentance is as central to Luke's missiology as is the reign of God or the concept of salvation. Of the fifty-six times the words "repent" or "repentance" occur in the New Testament, twenty-five are in Luke (Brunt: 29). He emphasizes it more than any other author.

"Repent" and "repentance" are often closely linked to "sinners"[5] and "forgiveness" in Luke. Thus John Brunt says, "To repent is to refocus one's life on God's plan and purpose. It means recognizing that we are sinners, that God has provided for our salvation in Jesus Christ, and that God, therefore, has a claim on our lives" (30).

But for Luke, repentance goes beyond a personal refocusing or redirection of one's life from sin to God. To have forgiveness has wider implications in Luke's soteriology. The word "forgiveness" (Greek: *aphesis*)[6] has a wide range of meaning: freeing bonded slaves, cancellation of monetary debts, eschatological liberation, and forgiveness of an individual's sins (Bosch, 1991:33).

When thinking of repentance, most believers focus on the cross and the atoning sacrifice of Jesus Christ. This has given rise to the question as to whether the theology of the cross in Luke has any atoning significance. Some say no. Michael Green, however, believes this to be "too rash a conclusion to draw from the fact that nowhere does Luke specifically say that forgiveness comes to men [only] through the cross" (73). For Green, it is clear that in the writings of Luke, the crucified and risen Christ is the one who gives forgiveness (296, note 183).

We miss Luke's point, however, if we attempt to impose a theology of atonement upon his work. Luke does not focus on an atonement theology as Paul does—a theology that some think is almost totally centered in the cross. Luke's theology is more wholistic as it treats reconciliation, repentance, and forgiveness.

Early in Luke's Gospel, the multidimensional nature of repentance and forgiveness is implied. In the Benedictus of Zechariah, we hear his prophecy of John:

> And you, child, will be called the prophet of the Most
>   High;
>   for you will go before the Lord to prepare his
>   ways,
> to give knowledge of salvation to his people
>   by the forgiveness of their sins. (Luke 1:76-77)

These words of Zechariah have strong social and political overtones (as noted above; cf. 1:69-71). So it is logical to conclude that the reference to forgiveness and salvation in these verses should also have a social dimension. Indeed, this begins to happen in the narration of John's ministry.

John the Baptist's evangelism is summarized in Luke 3, where it is recorded that "he went into all the region around the Jordan, proclaiming a baptism of repentance for the forgiveness of sins" (3:3). At least two points demonstrate that this "release" or "forgiveness" (Greek: *aphesis*) of sins is part of Luke's social concern.

First, Tannehill notes that the context includes a quote from Isaiah 40:3-5. The scenes of road building are images for repentance, symbolized by heights and depths leveled, and crooked and rough ways smoothed. These recall the social and political reversal in Mary's Magnificat: the mighty are brought down, and the lowly are exalted (Luke 1:52; Tannehill, 1986:48).

Second and even more significant is Luke's unique presentation of the dialogue with the crowds that come out to be baptized. John tells them to "bear fruits worthy of repentance" (Luke 3:8).

> And the crowds asked him, "What then should we do?" In reply he said to them, "Whoever has two coats must share with anyone who has none; and whoever has food must do likewise." Even tax collectors came to be baptized, and they asked him, "Teacher, what should we do?" He said to them, "Collect no more than the amount prescribed for you." Soldiers also asked him, "And we, what should we do?" He said to them, "Do not extort money from anyone by threats or false accusation, and be satisfied with your wages." (3:10-14)

Luke deliberately and uniquely wishes to link repentance with practical, social, down-to-earth behavior and response. The social implication of the Gospel is exceedingly strong here (Tienou: 266; Brunt: 33-34).

In Luke, furthermore, John the Baptist's message and ministry sets the tone for the ministry of Jesus and his followers. Repentance, forgiveness, and release from sin continues to be part of the message of Jesus and that of his followers; with the same social force as it is in John's message and evangelistic thrust.

We keep coming back to Luke 4:18, because this is a key verse in the development of Luke's wholistic theology and missiology. It, therefore, should not surprise us to find that *forgiveness* or *release* figures prominently in this pericope. Twice the word (*aphesis*) is used: first in the phrase "to proclaim release to the captives," and second in the last phrase "to let the oppressed go free." For Jesus, then, forgiveness in his evangelistic program includes this powerful social dimension, like John the Baptist's teaching.

We have argued that the release of the captives not only has implications for those held in demonic captivity, but also refers to those held in debtors' jail. If this is correct, then this forgiveness or release is certainly social. The same is true for the final phrase of the verse. Oppression here is primarily economic oppression. Jesus' mission is to give hope to the oppressed by announcing the inauguration of the Jubilee year (4:19). Forgiveness and release are definitely a social part of this new age.

Luke not only links release and forgiveness to socioeconomics but also to physical healing. The scenario of the healing of the paralytic (Luke 5:17-26) shows how he relates them closely. Jesus assures the paralytic that his sins are forgiven. The Pharisees and scribes protest, charging Jesus with blasphemy. In response Jesus says, "Which is easier, to say, 'Your sins are forgiven you,' or to say, 'Stand up and walk'? But so that you may know that the Son of Man has authority on earth to forgive sins, . . . I say to you, stand up and take your bed and go to your home" (5:23-24). Thus for Luke and Jesus, proclamation of forgiveness, release, and healing belong together (Bosch, 1989:11-12).

Another story is laced through with the theme of forgiveness: Jesus and the sinful woman at the Pharisee's house (Luke 7:36-50). This is an important account because it illustrates Luke's editorial work to make his point. The story is carefully placed in Luke (Matthew and Mark report a similar event at the close of Jesus' ministry). It is expanded to include the parable of two debtors and the forgiveness or cancellation of both debts.

The account is heavily focused on the outcast woman, who is not named, but simply identified as "a woman in the city, who was a sinner" (Luke 7:37), in contrast with the accepted-by-society Pharisee. Luke creatively relates all of this to emphasize his conception of release, forgiveness, and Jesus' attitude to women in particular, and to the outcast and marginal in general (cf. 7:33-35; Rice: 90-96).

This narrative comes soon after Jesus' response to John the Baptist's disciples: "Go and tell John" about the social and physical salvation they have seen (Luke 7:22-23). There is no direct reference to release from sins in this early passage. Yet there seems to be a close or even direct connection with 7:31-50. Both accounts center on the marginal and the outcast. The criticism of Jesus eating and being friends with tax collectors and sinners (7:31-35) leads into the story of the sinful woman at the Pharisee's house.

In this context, the story focuses on forgiveness. Jesus not only tells her that her sins are forgiven; he adds, "Your faith has saved you; go in peace" (Luke 7:50). Faith, salvation, forgiveness, release, social compassion for the outcasts—these all are part of a wholistic and rich tapestry that Luke weaves.

Much has been written about Matthew's great commission, but little is said about Luke's great commission in his Gospel. In his final words, Jesus charges his disciples:

> Thus it is written, that the Messiah is to suffer and to rise from the dead on the third day, and that repentance and forgiveness of sins is to be proclaimed in his

name to all nations, beginning from Jerusalem. You are witnesses of these things. And see, I am sending upon you what my Father promised; so stay here in the city until you have been clothed with power from on high. (Luke 24:46-49)

The central thrust of this commission is to proclaim repentance and forgiveness of sins. This is important in light of the fact that these concerns are found in a polymorphous form throughout the Gospel of Luke. David Bosch goes as far as to suggest that Luke's Gospel must be read and understood in light of this pericope (1991:91).

Robert Tannehill (1991:295-296) demonstrates how these verses closely connect basic statements concerning the mission of leading characters in Luke. Particularly, it seems to form an inclusio: the ministry of John the Baptist and the beginning of Jesus' ministry is the first term of the bracket, and the end of Jesus' earthly existence is the closing term of the bracket. The central focus is repentance and forgiveness.

Thus we find the proclamation of repentance and forgiveness or release from sin parallels Jesus' manifesto in the synagogue in Nazareth (Luke 4:18). But these words are even more precisely parallel with the description of John's evangelistic mission: repentance and forgiveness or release from sins (3:3).

Luke applies the term *release* or *forgiveness* (*aphesis*) to the missions of John in 3:3 and Jesus in 4:18. But then he does not use the term again until he describes the apostles' mission in 24:47 (Tannehill, 1991:296). This is not merely unreflective use of language; instead, Luke is quite intentional in so doing. For Luke, "repentance and forgiveness or release from sins" on the lips of Jesus in 24:47 should be understood in the same sense as Luke meant them at the beginning of his Gospel.

Luke's great commission thus serves as the hinge on which Acts hangs. Tannehill again demonstrates the parallel:

> The shared cluster of themes in Luke 24:47-49 and Acts 1:4-5, 8 indicates that the latter passage is repetitive. In both passages we find reference to Jerusalem as starting point, the apostles as witnesses, and the Spirit as promise and power. The mission of preaching to all nations in Luke 24:47 is expressed in Acts 1:8 as a command to be Jesus' witnesses "in Jerusalem, and in all Judea and Samaria, and to the ends of the earth.". . . . Repentance for release of sins is not mentioned in 1:8, but Peter's first sermon ends with an appeal to "repent and be baptized . . . in the name of Jesus Christ for the release of your sins" (2:38). (1986:296-297)

For Luke, then, these verses are vital in comprehending his theology and missiology. He does not present it as a mandate or command as Matthew presents his great commission. It is a promise, a fact (Bosch, 1991:91). So also, Acts 1:8 is not a command either, but a promise. The verb is indicative, not imperative (Gaventa: 416). But these promises, these facts, are intended to summarize Jesus' evangelistic mission as well as serving as a summary of what is to follow.

Peter's first evangelistic outreach and the response of the church (Acts 2) are significantly interrelated with John the Baptist's evangelistic proclamation and his response to the crowd (Luke 3). Peter is presented as a successor of John in preaching a message of repentance. John proclaimed a baptism of repentance for release or forgiveness of sins (Luke 3:3). Peter preaches, "Repent, and be baptized . . . so that your sins may be forgiven" (Acts 2:38).

John's preaching evoked the question, "What then should we do?" (Luke 3:10, 12, 14). In Acts, the crowd responded, "Brothers, what should we do?" (2:37).

Furthermore, there is a parallel between the narrative about John the Baptist, and the account of the primitive community having all things in common, selling their possessions and goods, and distributing the proceeds to all, as any had need (Acts 2:44-45). The story in Acts demonstrates a fulfillment, satisfying John's demand that sharing one's possessions demonstrates repentance (Luke 3:10-14; Tannehill, 1990:41). Acts 2:42-47 is definitely a description of the religious community life of those who respond to the call to repent and are baptized for the forgiveness of sins or release from sins.

Not only does Luke draw parallels between John the Baptist and Jesus and Peter; he also has a penchant for paralleling Paul with Peter. In Paul's final speech recorded in Acts, he summarizes his mission by quoting Christ's commission to him. In part, he is being sent to the Gentiles "to open their eyes so that they may turn from darkness to light and from the power of Satan to God, so that they may receive forgiveness of sins" (26:17-18).

Thus the tongues of John, Jesus, Peter, the apostles, and Paul give an emphasis on repentance and forgiveness and release from sins. In some cases the concept has clear social overtones; and they are all parallel. These facts demonstrate that Luke intends to paint a picture of repentance and forgiveness or release from sins which includes a social dimension throughout his entire work.

Conversion

Biblically, the distinction between repentance and conversion is minimal or even negligible. This is particularly true in Luke. Much of what was said above under the category of repentance is applicable here. However, I will treat these concepts separately and raise some issues not dealt with earlier. These issues focus more on the character of change as one becomes a believer.

One of the debatable questions, to which we believe Luke has an answer, is whether the change in conversion is punctiliar or linear. Some tend to define conversion as a moment of decision (punctiliar), or even a series of moments, such as conversion to Christ, conversion to the church, and conversion to the world. Others stress conversion as a process (linear), or deepening perception, reflection, and understanding.

We will not deny that the punctiliar understanding has biblical roots. But it is inadequate to limit conversion to that understanding of transformation or to make it even be the essential component A fundamental metamorphosis or paradigm shift must take place (Bosch, 1991:134-135), and it cannot be a matter of only a moment. Conversion is an ongoing and lifelong process.[7] It thus has a horizontal dimension which involves not only a point of turning *from*, but also a process of turning *to*.

An understanding of the biblical concept of *metanoia* supports our contention. *Metanoia*, regularly translated as "repentance," means a conversion that involves the total transformation of the attitudes and styles of life of a person or a group of persons.[8] In an Ecumenical Affirmation, the World Council of Churches correctly noted that conversion is furthermore "a dynamic and ongoing process which involves a turning from and a turning to. A turning from a life of sin and separation from God, to a life characterized by the forgiveness of sin, and obedience, and growth in Christ" (Stromberg: 19).

Luke's unique record of John the Baptist's evangelism supports our contention. He speaks about conversion by using the word *metanoeō*, "repent" (Luke 3:3). The conventional "change your mind" interpretation does not do justice to the context in which it occurs in 3:2-14. Even a cursory view of the dialogue clearly shows that one's actions, whether large or small, are most important in the conversion process. This is not merely a change of one's inner self or mind (cf. Schniewind: 270).[9]

We agree with Jim Wallis: *Metanoia* literally means

> to change the form, to turn the mind around, to take on a whole new identity. It means a transformation of life that is more basic, deeper, and more far-reaching than our common understanding of the word *repentance*. Our understanding of the word *repentance* carries a sense of guilt and being sorry for something. In sharp contrast, the Greek word *metanoia* speaks the language of transformation, meaning a change of orientation, character, and direction that is so pronounced and dramatic that the very form and purpose of a life is decisively altered, reshaped, and turned around. (1976:19-20)

This kind of transformation has personal, political, economic, and social consequences. Jesus says this kind of change is necessary for one to enter the reign of God.

It is this kind of change, however, which the rich ruler refuses to make (Luke 18:18-30). On the other hand, Luke juxtaposes the story of Zacchaeus (19:1-10) with that of the rich ruler to demonstrate how Zaachaeus' conversion involves a radical transformation of his relationship both with God and his fellow oppressed human beings. Conversion for Zacchaeus, an oppressive wealthy tax collector, means not only turning from his social sins and rejecting his past life of unjust oppression. It also means turning to a life which involves making restitution to those he defrauded, and sharing his possessions with the poor. Only then does Jesus announce, "Today salvation has come to this house" (19:9).

When we speak of conversion, then, we cannot focus solely on the turning *from*, particularly if that turning from is focused on cultural lifestyle. We need to concentrate more on the turning *to*, which means entering into a relationship with Christ and with his followers. The turning *from* must be, as in the case of Zacchaeus, a turning from ourselves and focusing on Christ and those around us. It is this paradoxical turning (cf. Potter: 317) that is conversion.

Conversion is a "paradigm shift," to borrow Thomas Kuhn's term, a change of perspective in which one enters a new personal relationship with Jesus and joins him and his community in the task of transforming the world. Conversion means that one enters into an ongoing process of incorporation into a new dimension of being in Christ and cooperating with him in the betterment of society.

Luke's presentation of John the Baptist and Zacchaeus makes it clear that conversion, repentance, and transformation do not take place in some personal mystical vacuum. The Baptist demands that his hearers bear "fruits" worthy of repentance; those fruits are social in their scope (Luke 3:8-14). They focus on the affluent sharing their surplus wealth with the poor. Those who gain their wealth by extortion should collect no more than that which is prescribed.

For Luke, this is as much the concrete and realistic implication of conversion as the so-called mystical turning to Jesus Christ. Persons are being transformed into citizens of the kingdom of Christ, and they will recognize that their transformation involves the pursuit of justice and equity in society.

The Holy Spirit

The Spirit is not particularly prominent in two of the three Synoptic Gospels: Matthew and Mark. But Luke's theology and missiology is undergirded by the Spirit. Luke has been called "the theologian of the Holy Spirit" (Bosch, 1991:113). The ministry of Jesus and his followers is initiated and guided by the Spirit. In Luke's writings, to evangelize (*euangelizein*) "is only possible when the Holy Spirit is present, at work, in action, and in control" (Barrett: 12).

Luke uniquely links the Spirit to mission (Bosch, 1991:114-115). In Paul's letters of thirty years earlier, the Holy Spirit was occasionally linked to mission. One hundred years later, the Holy Spirit was almost exclusively linked to sanctification and as a "guarantor of apostolicity." Today, more and more, we are recapturing Luke's emphasis on the role of the Holy Spirit in the evangelistic outreach of the community of believers.

A cursory view of Luke's volumes reveals the dominance of the Spirit.[10] Early in the Gospel, we find Elizabeth being filled with the Holy Spirit as she blesses Mary (1:41). So also is her husband as he blesses God in his famous Benedictus (1:67). Jesus is conceived by the Holy Spirit and Mary (1:35).

At Jesus' baptism, the same Spirit comes upon him (3:22)—a sign of ordination for ministry. Filled with the Holy Spirit, he goes into the wilderness, where he is tempted by the devil (4:1-2). The very Spirit is upon him when he leaves the desert and enters the synagogue of Nazareth to give his programmatic statement of mission (4:18). The Holy Spirit directs and empowers the ministry of Jesus.

That same Spirit is offered to those who ask the Father (11:13). As Jesus prepares to ascend into heaven, he reminds the disciples that he will send the Spirit to fulfill the Father's promise (Joel 2:28-32; Acts 2:1-21). The Spirit will clothe them with power to proclaim the gospel to all nations (Luke 24:47-48).

Luke begins his second volume with a reworked version of Jesus' promise. The Holy Spirit will descend upon them and give them power to witness (Acts 1:8). This begins to happen soon afterward; on the day of Pentecost they are filled with the Holy Spirit (2:1-4). On that day Peter preaches that they are experiencing a fulfillment of what Joel prophesied, an outpouring of the Spirit (2:17). So the crowds should respond positively by being baptized and receiving the gift of the Holy Spirit (2:38).

The Holy Spirit directs all aspects of the primitive church's ministry and mission. This includes Peter's detection of Ananias and Sapphira's lie to the Holy Spirit (Acts 5:3), selecting seven Hellenists "full of the Spirit" to perform special social services in the community (6:1-6), Philip's meeting with the Ethiopian eunuch (8:29), and setting apart Barnabas and Saul-Paul for their international missionary journey (13:2).

Luke also has the Spirit bringing resolution to the debate at the council of Jerusalem (Acts 15:28), and guiding Paul (by hindering and directing) to his first unplanned trip to Europe (16:6-10). For Luke, the Holy Spirit is a dominant force in the evangelistic and total mission enterprise of all the active participants in his two books.

Again notice the importance of Luke 4:18-19 in Luke's theology. As argued above, this passage is multidimensional in its understanding of mission, but with special focus on the social, including the physical and political. Jesus claims that the Spirit of the Lord is upon himself in his total ministry (4:18, 21). Hence, the Holy Spirit is the one at work also through Jesus' followers in any social action which initiates persons into the reign of God. The power of the Spirit is certainly at work in Jesus as he heals the sick and casts out unclean spirits. So also the Spirit is directing as Jesus announces good news to the poor and challenges those who oppress the outcast and marginal. And when the Seventy do the same things (10:1-20), Jesus rejoices "in the Holy Spirit" (10:21).

Neither can we overemphasize the importance of Luke's focus on the end of Jesus' earthly existence and the beginning of the mission of the primitive church. Already we have noted the significance of Luke 24:47-49 and Acts 1:8. The Spirit becomes the catalyst and the driving and guiding force in mission in which repentance and forgiveness of sins are the focal point. This is central to the apostles' and primitive church's witness from Jerusalem to the ends of the earth. The Spirit then not only inspires bold preaching and the performance of signs and wonders, but also the taking care of each others' needs and devotion to one another.

In Luke-Acts, evangelistic outreach is only possible by the power of the Holy Spirit. John the Baptist, Jesus, and his followers, including the early apostolic church—all were endowed with and inspired by the Spirit. Therefore, the Holy Spirit empowers and leads all evangelism—personal and social, physical and political; and all dimensions of evangelism—salvation, repentance, conversion, and so on. All these are valid in the process of initiating people into the reign of God only if the Holy Spirit is at the heart and center of that evangelism.

5

Missiological Implications

Thus far I have attempted to demonstrate two things. First, a functional definition of evangelism should not be limited to Matthew's great commission, or even to a Pauline practice as illustrated in his epistles. Other biblical documents and narratives can and do present us with evangelistic paradigms from which we can draw for use in contemporary contexts.

Second, I have argued that evangelism is wholistic in the theology of Luke, as he portrays the ministry of John the Baptist, Jesus, his followers, and the early church. This wholism has a strong social component that has been missing for most of the twentieth century in evangelical Christianity. Too often evangelism has been incomplete.

This chapter furthers the recovery of missing components of evangelism. It does so on one hand by rejecting the reductionism of fundamentalist evangelicalism, and on the other hand by positively projecting Luke's wholism into current mission.

In doing the latter, we recognize that we cannot apply Luke's account of the words and ministry of the varied evangelists (such as John the Baptist, Jesus, Peter) on a one-for-one basis in our times. We are in different worlds, different contexts. Neither should we simply deduce principles. In my second chapter, on "Hermeneutical Method" (above), I demonstrated the difficulties one faces when such approaches are followed. Instead, we need to appropriate the biblical text in imaginative and creative ways which are appropriate to our unique self-definition— which must also remain fundamentally true to the whole gospel of Jesus Christ.

Doing this wholistic appropriation is a daunting task, due to strong opposition from forces that wish to limit the enterprise. We first must address the debate that arises from this opposition by showing that a limited definition of evangelism is certainly contrary to Luke's paradigm.[1]

Evangelism: The Debate

Earlier in this book, we defined evangelism as an invitation and an initiation into the reign of God. The enterprise is complex, multidimensional, and polymorphous. The reign of God is not limited to one state or place; nor does it impinge only upon the individual and a spiritual dimension of life. On the contrary, it impacts all contemporary living as well as future dimensions of salvation.

Yet many evangelical Christians limit evangelism to one or more of the following tasks: (1) "soul-winning," converting persons so that they verbally acknowledge Jesus as Lord and Savior, and/or become members of a church; (2) church planting; (3) "witness," verbally sharing one's personal faith in Jesus in a fairly narrow spiritual sense; (4) public proclamation of the gospel in traditional categories; and (5) personal discipleship, mostly in the sense of abstaining from a select list of sins. Generally, in none of these is a wider social definition considered.

There are several reasons why the social aspect has been ignored or at least downplayed. First, many fundamentalist evangelicals continue to associate social ministries with the modernist controversy, liberalism, and the social gospel of the early twentieth century. Addressing this, William Pannell notes that many evangelical evangelists react negatively to the social-gospel mystique—even though they have not read Walter Rauschenbusch's social theology. They fear that if it is taken seriously, a "bastardization of the true gospel will result, and, *viola*, we'll all become liberals!" (12-13).

The first reason many evangelicals reject the social component of evangelism seems political; the second is theological. Prophetic interpretation and futuristic eschatology prevent them from perceiving a more wholistic understanding. Dispensationalists are a case in point. George Peters in his work *A Biblical Theology of Missions* gives us a glimpse of this perspective. His dispensationalist presuppositions lead him to argue that the cultural (or social) and evangelistic mandates are not on equal terms.

Peters even claims that the social aspect is not in the mission of the church at all:

> I do not find anywhere in the Bible that the first mandate comes under the biblical category of missions. It is man's assignment as man and is to be fulfilled on the human level. It is not implied in the Great Commissions of our Lord to his disciples, nor do any of the spiritual gifts (charismata) as presented in the Scriptures relate to it. It is therefore unscriptural to confuse these two mandates and speak of them on equal terms as missions and church ministries. (40)

This statement is typical for many evangelicals and normative because it limits the mission and evangelistic demand to a certain reading of Matthew and Paul. Yet it totally ignores the Lukan paradigm and may indeed misinterpret Matthew and Paul.

George Peters does have a social conscience, and he recognizes that true Christians will have such. Yet it will not be explicitly manifested in this dispensation. He makes it plain that the reign of God has social implications. But this is only through the ministry of individual Christians and "the general impact of the gospel upon the conscience of society."

The presence of the gospel in society "constitutes judgment, modification, and enrichment of the order of society. It is strongly social in its general impact, regulating all relationships according to the will and purpose of God." But although these implications are "present within the individual, within the Christian church, and within the providential government of God in this dispensation, its full manifestation is futuristic" (Peters: 41).

This futuristic eschatology leads many Christians to totally reject most present social responsibility, particularly in the area of justice. Their supreme task is the future eternal salvation of the sinner. They have a pessimistic worldview. The present world is evil. Injustice and other such social issues are only signs of Christ's imminent return.

In reaction to this pessimism and fatalism, Tom Sine relates a personal incident followed by a logical comment:

> While I was making a presentation on world hunger
> at a Christian college, a student began waving her
> hand. I finally stopped and said, "What is it?" She responded, "Do you have any idea of what you said?" I
> replied, "I don't know, tell me." She said, "You said
> we should feed hungry people, . . . if we feed hungry
> people, then things won't get worse, and if things

don't get worse, then Jesus won't come." The logic of
that viewpoint would lead us to torpedo the grain
boats going to Africa while saying, "Even so, come
quickly, Lord Jesus!" (28; also Bosch, 1983:277).[2]

This deterministic view of history and pessimistic view
of the present and future has been used as an excuse for
Christians not to be involved in social action. Like dis-
obedient Jonah (4:1-11), believers with this view seem
more eager for God's judgment to fall than for people to
experience the fullness of God's grace. But such a view is
unbiblical—at least if we use Luke as a paradigm for Christian existence. It is based on a too-narrow reading of
selected biblical texts, at the expense of texts that do not fit
the mold. There may be a mixture of truth and error in
what is affirmed; but it certainly is a stupendous error for
such Christians to deny the social dimension of mission.

A third reason for the rejection of the social dimension
of evangelism is pragmatic. This is closely associated with
the church-growth school founded by Donald McGavran.
The school arose out of a pragmatic conclusion: God wills
that churches grow numerically. Churches that were involved in social concern were not growing; on the other
hand, numerical growth was seen in conservative churches which rejected the social gospel and embraced an individualistic, personal-salvation gospel.

Although most church-growth practitioners will agree
that their missiology is pragmatic, they just as strongly argue that it is theological. McGavran sets forth his position
that "mission[3] must be what God desires. It is . . . *missio
Dei*, the mission of God. . . . What kind of mission does *he*
desire? For that is what mission essentially and theologi-
cally is" (20). For McGavran, the two choices of what God
desires are: (1) good works, and (2) reconciling men and
women to God in Christ. But which comes first?

As to the first choice, he notes that so great is the number of calls for social needs that Christians can lose their way among them and see them all equally as mission. Therefore, the question of priorities can't be avoided. And good works must not take priority. Instead, God wills the second choice to take priority. It is God's will that lost persons be found, that they be reconciled to God. God's overriding desire is that human beings be redeemed. He wants to find the lost. "Social service pleases God, but it must never be substituted for finding the lost. Our Lord did not rest content with feeding the hungry and healing the sick," says McGavran (21-22).

In a number of areas, McGavran's assumptions are weak because of what they ignore. In the first place, to limit social concern to "good works" is to miss the biblical understanding of the concept. While it includes giving of gifts and *doing* good works, it has to do both with attitude and action.

Second, God does will that persons be reconciled to him. But reconciliation is wholistic. God wishes to find and save whole persons. The lost are not only those who are so-called "spiritually" lost. It is sad that we read the Lukan parables (especially in Luke 15) so narrowly and lose sight of their social context. In numerous instances, the lost for Luke were "sinners" (a technical term) and tax collectors, for example. These were social outcasts. Jesus reached them personally and socially.

Third, McGavran is correct that Jesus did not rest content with feeding the hungry and healing the sick. However, McGavran fails to recognize that Jesus also did not rest content with saving people's "souls"! We do agree with him (with definitional qualifications) that service must not be so disproportionately emphasized at the expense of verbal witness that findable people are continually being lost because of incomplete communication of the gospel.

But again, our emphasis would be on the word "dispro-portionately." This concern for balance can apply to all dimensions of evangelism.

However, the church-growth school does not see it thus. Instead, they argue philosophically that in proportioning social ministries alongside church planting, the degree of growth achieved must be taken into account. "The chief and irreplaceable purpose of mission is church growth," argues McGavran (1990:22). Finally, it is this pragmatic consideration that counts.

McGavran does suggest that occasionally for limited times, social concerns may be assigned a higher priority and receive greater attention than what he calls evangelism, such as in the civil rights movement in the 1960s (22-23; see Wagner: 108). McGavran, however, has not given a basis for determining how and under what circumstances the priorities should be reversed. Why, we ask, is the issue of poverty today not as acute as that of racism in the 1960s? Is the concern of family breakdown serious enough to reverse the priorities? These and many similar questions are left unanswered.

As we showed in our first chapter, the broad consensus among evangelical leaders today is to make personal evangelism primary, following the 1974 Lausanne Covenant. Many fall in the above categories who either totally reject Christian social involvement or minimize it to one extent or the other. There are others, however, who attempt to avoid the prioritization and yet still maintain the distinction.

In his look at *One-Sided Christianity*, Ronald Sider shows that evangelism and social responsibility are intertwined and related. But he argues that they must not be equated or confused one with the other. In chapter nine of his book, he is at pains to distinguish evangelism from social action. "In evangelism," he writes, "the central intention is to lead non-Christians to become disciples of Jesus Christ. In social action, the central intention is to improve the socioeconomic or psychological well-being of people for their life here on earth" (163).

However, his arguments are based on a narrow definition of salvation (which he spells out in the appendix). For Sider, salvation is what happens when a person accepts Christ and joins the Christian community, and also what happens when Christ renews the cosmos at his return. He contends that all other restoration is social justice, not salvation (199-213). Yet this distinction does not negate his position that traditional evangelism and social concern must be a fifty-fifty combination.

There are others like Harvie Conn who use the metaphor "two sides of the same coin" to describe the relationship between evangelism and social ministries (1982:9). They are interdependent and constantly interacting. Delos Miles adds other metaphors: "Evangelism and social involvement are two wings of the same gospel bird. . . . Evangelism is surely blood brother to social involvement" (7). Miles feels strongly that social involvement is not a distraction from evangelism. But he does not believe that it should ever become equivalent to evangelism (22).

While Miles's arguments are valuable in moving toward a biblically wholistic concept of evangelism, he makes some awkward definitional distinctions. For example, he separates social ministry from social action. Social ministry includes feeding the hungry, giving drink to the thirsty, welcoming strangers, clothing the naked, visiting the sick and prisoners (Matthew 25:31-46). Social action involves "self-conscious attempts to change sinful social structures." It includes "deeds of love and justice on behalf of society's outcast and under class. Such actions may range all the way from passing a resolution to participating in an armed revolution," according to Miles (160).

I am not convinced with this distinction nor in admitting armed revolution as appropriate for a follower of Christ, the Prince of Peace. Miles preserves the idea that the caring for the needy is biblical and social action is not. I believe that both caring for the needy and confronting sinful social structures are ministries and demand our action, but not with physical violence.

The same critique holds for Miles's definition of evangelism: "being, doing, and telling the gospel of the kingdom of God, in order that by the power of the Holy Spirit persons and structures may be converted to the lordship of Jesus Christ" (14). We would argue that such "being and doing" should include social concern and action.

Even evangelicals like Delos Miles who make a theoretical distinction between evangelism and social concern admit that it is truly hard to draw a line separating evangelism and social involvement in Jesus' statement of mission in Luke 4:18-19. It is clear that in this passage, Jesus interprets his mission in social terms (33).

Lesslie Newbigin's comments, like those of Miles, are close to where I stand. He argues that no priority should be assigned between evangelism and social action, "because each without the other is ultimately vain. . . . The deed without the word is dumb, and the word without the deed is empty." In a significant contribution, Newbigin suggests, "The dichotomy that opens up in our perception at this point is part of the deep-going dualism that we inherit from the pagan (Greek) roots of our culture and which the biblical witness has never been able to eradicate" (1982:146).

Yet Newbigin avoids the term *wholistic evangelism* and prefers to use the term *evangelism* exclusively for the action of verbal proclamation in which Jesus' name is central (1982:149). But what Newbigin and others fail to recognize is that in wholistic evangelism, Jesus' name and person must always be central in all aspects of the enterprise. However, Newbigin rejects the label *wholistic evangelism* "not only because he thinks it confuses two distinct things, but because it allows the telling of the good news to be sidestepped in favor of social reform. The latter, he says, is equally an obligation and should not be substituted for the verbal witness (1982:154).

In his definition of evangelism, Newbigin raises an issue which we need reexamine. He claims that evangelism is verbal proclamation. Possibly most evangelicals define it that way to clarify it as separate from other activities of the church. Thus one can speak of the "evangelistic ministry of the church." Some would say, "If everything is evangelism, then nothing is evangelism."[4]

However, I feel that this common tendency to reduce evangelism to proclamation is inadequate and an artificial limitation. Evangelism must include other elements of Christian initiation. The work of the evangelist spills over into other activities besides proclamation (see Abraham: 55; cf. Brueggemann: 37).

If we do speak of "proclamation" in the context of evangelism, we must realize that it is "not the act of proclamation *per se*, but the message being proclaimed" (Abraham: 59). It is a message which not only includes "spiritual words" but "social deeds." If we make a dichotomy between words and deeds even in the definition of evangelism, we succumb to the Western and Greek dualism which Newbigin himself warns us against.

I recognize that we are fighting an uphill battle. The persuasive influence of Western dualism and individualism is so great that it is almost impossible for many who are steeped in such a tradition to conceive of any other worldview. In the Western worldview, the spiritual and the social should not mix, nor should the personal and the public. But this outlook, which then disassociates the "gospel" from the world and which declares that salvation is spiritual and transcendent, denies "the incarnational essence of the faith" (Watson, 1983:6).[5]

I am convinced, more so after a careful rereading of Luke's work, that the reign of God is not spiritualized in Scripture nor is it limited to the so-called spiritual side of the human being. When dealing with the reign of God or salvation experience, we must not make a separation of the inward and spiritual from the outward, visible, public, and social (Verkuyl: 197-198; Newbigin, 1986:97).

My argument goes beyond simply a neo-individualism which challenges the "individual" to be socially concerned for the "individual" neighbor. It implies the public, the political. Some claim that the church should not be involved in politics because the only business of the church is the eternal salvation of the individual soul. However, this is based on a long-standing heretical dichotomy held by sincere religious persons.

As Richard Mouw argues in his book *Political Evangelism*, evangelism must be concerned with the proclamation and demonstration of the full gospel. It must take place on every front and be directed to all dimensions of human life. It must address liberation even in the area of public policy and political institutions (cf. World Council of Churches: 28; Newbigin, 1986:96).

I am arguing for a *complete evangelism*, with all its parts. The only way the conclusions presented here can be understood is if philosophically there is an acceptance of this wholistic worldview. Newbigin says it well: "The whole of experience in the natural world, in the world of public affairs of politics, economics and culture, and the world of inward spiritual experience is to be seen as one whole in the light of [the] disclosure of the character and will of its Creator" (1986:89).

Evangelism then does not consist of proclamation and

verbal witness only. It involves word and deed, proclamation and presence, explanation and example, public and private, political and personal, spiritual and social. It cannot be limited to winning "souls." The emphasis should not be solely on the inward and spiritual side of the individual. To say that the major concern of the church is the nonmaterial aspect of life, the "spiritual," is to be Gnostic, says Bosch (1987:100). And it is also Gnostic for us to try to prioritize, placing the "inner soul" of the poor, marginal, and outcast on a higher pedestal than their physical bodies and emotional well-being.

Hence, I mostly agree with Emilio Castro:

> We must say no to any attempts to permanently prioritize the ways and means of obedience in the service of the kingdom. The only priority is the kingdom, the King, and his invitation of love. And the word spoken and a glass of cold water given in Jesus' name are both, depending on the circumstances, correct entry points into the total dynamic of the kingdom. There can be no gospel of individual salvation without reference to the justice of the kingdom. There is no love of God unrelated to my neighbor. The encounter between church members and persons outside the Christian community is, *de facto*, a total encounter where words receive meaning from the entire behavior of the Christian community. We cannot decide whether our neighbor is saved; that *needs* to wait for the final surprise of the Last Judgement (Matt. 7:21-23; 25:31-46). We proclaim salvation *in* Christ. That means salvation in his plan to transform all reality. So any word that announces the gospel is an entry point into the total kingdom; if not it is not an authentic proclamation of the gospel. And no Christian solidarity with the poor can exist which does not point to the

totality the kingdom promises, including the invitation to personal faith and witness (10).[6]

So what is God's desire for the world? What is the ultimate goal of the *missio Dei*, the mission of God? It is that all be reconciled into his reign. And not only *all*, as in all individuals, but all aspects of the individual, and all things which impinge upon the individual in community. Evangelists are therefore challenged by the missiology of Luke. The books of Luke-Acts show that John, Jesus, and the early Christian community participated in the *missio Dei* wholistically.

They gave hope to the spiritually and socially outcast and marginal; they challenged and were sensitive to the personal and the social sins. They would not cut asunder what God had joined together (Potter, 1968:177; Watson. 1985:219). Evangelists today must also keep the marriage intact Let us, then, explore evangelism today by using the Lukan paradigm of hope and challenge.

The Lukan Paradigm

We are faced by a bleak reality in North American Christianity, even in evangelical Christianity: we are turned off by evangelism. Among most Christians, evangelism has therefore taken a backseat and become a low-priority agenda item, and some even make straightforward objections to it.

As far as nonchurched persons are concerned, they are turned off because religion has been preached at them and pushed upon them. They are treated as an evangelistic project rather than as a person (Pippert: 16).

What are some of the obstacles which make evangelism such a low priority in North America? Charles Van Engen, in his book *You Are My Witnesses*, discusses a number of cultural and ecclesiastical obstacles (1992:3-7). First, our culture to a large degree is self-sufficient and really doesn't need God's help. Second, we are culturally brainwashed to separate the private and the public, and issues of faith are thought to belong to the private sphere. Thus traditional evangelism, being so public, seems to be at odds with private religion. Third, our culture feels no need for radical conversion.

In the churches, there are a couple of obstacles, according to Van Engen. First, believers have a basic lack of clarity about the task. Second, what is being shared in our evangelism is unclear.

Charles Scriven, a Seventh-Day Adventist theologian, goes beyond these two churchy obstacles and discusses four objections against evangelism raised by thoughtful Christians. (1) Relativity: Many argue that no person or institution can claim ultimate truth. (2) Autonomy: This Western philosophy states that mature people should choose their own way of life for themselves, based on careful independent thinking, without the direction of anyone else. (3) Hypocrisy: The church cannot recommend its message to others until it gets its own house in order. (4) Irrelevancy, possibly the greatest obstacle and objection for the modern person: In what way does the gospel really make a difference? (1988a:22-28).

These are all valid and reasonable objections; much could be written to explicate them and respond to them. But the simple fact is that almost all of them are based on a narrow view of evangelism. It is our contention that if the Lukan paradigm of evangelism is recaptured, many of these obstacles can be surmounted. The narrow vision of evangelism needs to be replaced with a broad, wholistic, humanizing, conscientizing, liberating, engaging, and challenging one. Such a complete evangelism addresses all dimensions of life in a relevant and meaningful way.

In the earlier chapter on hermeneutics, I said it would be unwise simply to apply the biblical text directly to any particular contemporary situation. Yes, we must reenact the drama as we "do the text" (Brueggemann: 8). But it must be appropriated in new, creative, and relevant ways. In some cases, the text has fairly exact parallels in our twentieth-century societies. In others, that is not the case.

For example, the situation in a poor Jamaican town may parallel more closely a town in first-century Palestine than a town in suburbia Seattle. The U.S. Northwest evangelical, therefore, needs to struggle to find ways to address the spiritual and social problems as part of the invitation for persons to enter the reign of God.

Tom Sine is one of the contemporary writers and evangelical practitioners challenging us to find new ways in approaching this wholistic evangelistic enterprise. In his book *Taking Discipleship Seriously* (9 ff.), he discusses several global and national changes which modern Christian disciples of Jesus have a duty to address, especially as we approach the twenty-first century.

Among the global issues are international poverty, urban crowding, environmental degradation, political destabilization, and population growth. The national issues include demographic changes, racial concerns, working families' problems, inner city challenges, bioethics, and technological issues.

Brueggemann's list complements Sine's: economic questions in the two-thirds world, sexual intimacy, family-life crises, local and international security, inter-generational conflicts, and problems of homelessness (41). To these can be added all the personal and spiritual challenges detailed in numerous traditional evangelistic books.

With a list like this, the evangelical Christian's hands will be filled as evangelistic tasks are engaged. All aspects of society will be engaged. Roy Adams, an associate editor of the *Adventist Review,* in 1994 wrote that as Christians wait for the second coming of Christ, we should not become "dropouts from society—detached passivists, heavenly minded zombies, completely out of touch with the realities of temporal society. Rather, we should become appropriately engaged with the issues and concerns of our time" (5). Jesus included an apt command in the parable of the pounds: "Do business with these until I come back," or "Occupy till I come" (Luke 19:13, NRSV/KJV).

Hope

To evangelize in today's society, we must do what Luke has the Jesus movement doing: giving hope and presenting challenge, incorporating reconciliation and justice. The hope which needs to be proclaimed and demonstrated is not merely futuristic. Luke (like the rest of the New Testament authors) has shown us that the reign of God is not reducible to a moment in history or some localized set of circumstances, cosmic or earthly. The reign of God is present, and yet its glorious consummation is future.

The reign of God is a metaphor for a quality of life both here and in the hereafter. Present experiences, then, can be part of God's reign. We know we live in a world of sin, suffering, and death in all their aspects. However, we not only look forward to future perfect consummation; there is also hope that in the present we can enter the reign of God in all its dimensions.

Part of the aim of evangelism, then, is to give present hope, today, to those who are suffering under the weight of sin in all its forms. We need to invite the sufferer, through proclamation and action, word and deed, into the reign of God. To put it another way, the aim of evangelism is the establishment of shalom, wholeness. This is a shalom that is more than personal salvation. Peace, integrity, community, harmony, and justice are all wholly incorporated in it.

This shalom is announced in the *kērygma*, proclamation; it is lived in *koinonia*, fellowship and sharing with each other; it is demonstrated in *diakonia*, humble service to others. These three—kērygma, koinonia, and diakonia—should all be integrated into evangelism's shalom, says Hoekendijk (25). All these of necessity are part of the hope which Jesus brings to humanity now. They are part of his redeeming and transforming presence in history. We are called upon to participate with Christ in this hope-giving, transforming, reconciling enterprise.

If we claim that Jesus' agenda for the reign of God is at the center of our lives, then his agenda for the poor as presented in the synagogue in Nazareth should be our agenda. We are called to proclaim good news to the poor; we are called to make a difference now in the lives of the economically marginal people in society. Leonardo Boff is perceptive in noting that the continuing poverty of the poor betrays the failure of traditional evangelism. A new evangelization is needed which proclaims the good news of liberation (1).

Good news to the poor involves compassion, mercy, economic well-being, and transformation. For them to experience the present fullness of God's reign, they have to enjoy the dignity of being human and in relationship with those already experiencing the material blessings of the reign. Such a ministry can best be accomplished when we are incarnated with the poor, when we enter into their lives.

This is uncomfortable; this is difficult; but it is necessary, as Mary Motte says:

> It is not easy to enter into the lives of the poor, but unless one enters their lives, one cannot engage in a dia-

logue that will articulate the message of the good
news of God's love. It is by entering into the situation
of the poor that the person at the service of universal
mission shares in a dialogue communicating good
news. Each instance of such a dialogue replicates that
begun in the Incarnation, when God in Jesus Christ
humbly entered the human condition, and began a
conversation expressed in human love and caring, a
service of washing another's feet. (54)

The result of this incarnational experience with the
poor will be to build their self-worth, human dignity, relationships, and community. That will spin off into economic well-being. But it also provides the basis for communicating in verbal and actual ways how much God loves
them and desires them to fully enter his reign now.

The hope given by Jesus and his followers involved a
healing ministry. His manifesto in Nazareth included giving sight to the blind and releasing the captives—metaphors for all his healing activities. How can we appropriate
this in our contemporary evangelistic task? Many evangelical Christians are hesitant about involving healing and
deliverance from demonic forces in any evangelistic efforts. And yet we cannot deny that as far as Luke is concerned, they are inexorably linked in Jesus' ministry.

As mentioned earlier, "Jesus' healing activity demonstrated that the saving grace of God extends not only to
personal guilt and broken relationships but to human bodies, to societal structures, to mysterious forces that hold
creation in check" (Senior: 151). The healing is a metaphor
for comprehensive wholeness: physical, religious, and social.

There is much more to healing than treating people's
organs and bodies. The whole person needs healing—
minds, emotions, attitudes, and souls. Salvation needs to

extend to the healing of relationships in the family and community. This means restoring human wholeness. The reign of God is a reign of shalom: "of total interrelatedness, of total harmony and well-being, of peace, and wholeness" (Arias: 76).

Christians may use avenues of prayer, medicine, pastoral counseling, group therapy, nutrition, mental health services, rehabilitation from drug addiction, social reconciliation, and the defense of human rights in any form. Thus, according to Arias, the healing ministry of the contemporary church is not merely a secondary social service but certainly "an inseparable part of the announcement of the good news of the kingdom of life revealed in Jesus Christ" (75).

A complete evangelism includes the healing of day-to-day problems; caring for personal, mental, and physical frailties; being involved with the intimate experiences of our neighbors; restoring good community relations; and so on. In these ministries, we contribute toward accomplishing our evangelistic mission.

As Charles Van Engen rightly says, "Matters related to possessions, finances, ambitions, fears, children, sex, marriage, death, physical fitness, jobs, schools—all of these are subjects which can trigger an appropriate word, an act of love and concern, a sharing of the grace of God with our neighbors. Faith must be relevant" (1992:36).

This aspect of evangelism embraces all the hopes, the longings, the anguished cries of people—whether those cries be spiritual, social, physical, or political. They are cries which need attention. The criers need healing, liberation, and transformation as part of entering into the reign of God. The evangelistic task must then entail

the carrying out of God's works by service to individuals, groups, and societal structures in temporal need.

> The works of God are the works of justice and compassion, whereby men and women are liberated here and now from the immediate hardship of injustices and are thereby enabled to experience what is truly a certain beginning of the liberating of God's full kingdom. . . . By his cures Jesus saves (*sōzein*) both the spiritual (pardon for sin and assurance of grace) and earthly (physical ailments). He reinstates or reconciles the marginal or banned persons into the social and religious community of Israel. (Stransky: 347)

In giving hope and healing to the poor, the outcast, the weak, the marginal, the sinner, and the sick—we empower them "to lift up their heads and hold them high, to recognize their own dignity, to begin to see themselves in a new light" (Bosch, 1989:8). A transformation takes place. But it is not merely a social transformation; it is one in which Christ is encountered and recognized as the one who gives hope, healing, and salvation. Christ is and must always be the focal center of this evangelistic enterprise in its totality.

Challenge

Whenever evangelism is reduced to only the dimension of giving hope, or simply the presentation of a spiritualized gospel of personal salvation, without challenging evil and the forces behind all evil—it is not evangelism. Instead, to use Bosch's term, it is "counter-evangelism" (1987:102).

Jesus not only gave hope and good news, but also challenged the people and the structures of first-century Palestine. Likewise, we his followers must today challenge the religious, economic, political, moral, and all social structures and practices which war against the reign of God. This is *prophetic evangelism.*

The opposite of this is *evangelism of conformity,* which "provides no challenge to the dominant social, economic, and political values of a society, but, rather, operates within the framework and consensus of those values" (Wallis, 1976:24). Prophetic evangelism challenges people to take stock of their lives in radical ways to seek God's will.[7]

Prophetic evangelism includes denouncement and call. An example of denouncement is the censuring of the world's oppressive systems, such as the imbalance of the wealth and power concentrations versus the poverty and powerlessness in the world (Watson, 1983:7). The call is for persons, communities, and societies to repent and be converted. Prophetic evangelism is "at once a denouncement of the impugnment of [God's] sovereignty by human sin and a pronouncement of the saving presence of God's love and justice" (1983:7).

This prophetic form of evangelism need not be exclusively public in its outreach. Private conversation is as valid a forum as the public challenge. However, prophetic evangelism must be implemented as continuously as the more "acceptable" methods, regardless of the response it evokes. It must deal with sin in whatever form it raises its head.

Jim Wallis notes that

> the scope of our evangelism must be at least as pervasive as the power of sin itself. As sin and death manifest themselves institutionally, politically, and economically as well as personally, our evangelism must bring the gospel into active confrontation with the personal and corporate character and dimension of sin and death. (1976:31-32)

Evangelism must deal with social and systemic sins as well as any sins that are at odds with the reign of God. Peo-

ple need to be saved not only from personal sins but from
social sins. The gospel challenges contemporary evangelism to realize this broader perspective of evangelism, says
David Watson. "The gospel for sinner *and* sinned against,
[must] be incorporated into an evangelistic message
which goes beyond personal conviction, repentance, forgiveness, and regeneration, to a global hope and vision: a
message for human systems as well as human beings; a
hope for human history as well as human souls"
(1985:219-220).

The difficulty with this dimension of evangelism in our
society is that it is both religiously and socially countercultural, and thus evokes negative responses. Yet we are
called to be a contrast community, against any sin
entrenched in cultures. Jesus called his disciples to be
countercultural in this way. His call was for them to be radically counter to the prevailing culture of that time on matters that were oppressive and unfair when tested by his
gospel. He called his followers to be radically transformed
and to challenge the fundamental values and life's priorities in their society (Sine: 19). This produced conflict then,
as it will now. The gospel will always produce a negative
response by those who resist its truth.

The presentation of the whole gospel will by its very
nature produce conflict. It is what Brueggemann calls
being "epistemologically subversive." The gospel is
"affrontive to liberal and conservative alike, because the
claims are too radical for liberals and too comprehensive
for conservatives" (38). The language of the gospel is
"brusque, harsh, and not 'user-friendly.' It follows . . . that
such a claim requires in most of our churches, liberal and
conservative, a changed universe of discourse to permit
the dramatic power of the claim to be either spoken or
heard" (38-40).

Our evangelism, then, will of necessity be confrontational, as Jesus' evangelization was confrontational. Just as Jesus' evangelism was a threat to the established order, so ours will be. The presentation of the reign of God will always produce intense reactions, pro and con. "It attracts and repels at the same time" (Arias: 43).

According to Luke, one major (if not *the* major) area which Jesus had to challenge was that of socioeconomics. In similar and different ways, this same major area has been left untackled by most evangelicals. Brueggemann discusses this at length in his book *Biblical Perspectives on Evangelism*, noting that in our culture and in our churches, "death operates in the seductive power of consumer economics with its engines of greed" (40). It is so pervasive that it has exercised sovereignty over most of our lives. Thus the central conflict with the gospel in our time has to do with socioeconomics.

Brueggemann is quick to note that by tilting the gospel toward socioeconomics and political matters, he is not introducing a "liberal" category. In fact, throughout Scriptures "the gospel has been exactly and precisely concerned with social relations related to power, goods, and access. . . . The issue, however, is not finally socioeconomic or political. It is theological. It concerns the power for life and the power for death" (40-41), and the struggle between them.

To appropriate the gospel in our context, we are challenged to find ways to "disengage our life, our bodies, and our imagination from the seemingly all-powerful world of consumer pursuits" (Brueggeman: 42). We are challenged to disengage our middle and upper-class lifestyles and their implications. Each of us must give up the cultural values of looking out for myself as number one. The cultural right of getting a piece of the great American pie must be removed from the center of our lives. All these secular values which reign supreme—materialism, individualism, and self-seeking—must be dethroned (Sine: 40).

Delos Miles is poignant:

> If we practice prophetic evangelism, we shall call all
> persons including ourselves, to turn from their wick-
> ed ways. We shall condemn economic oppression as
> strongly as we do rape. God never intended that we
> grow fat and sleek while kids starve. Stealing persons'
> dignity is as bad as armed robbery. Prophetic evange-
> lism tells persons they don't have to get rich or get
> even in order to have the good life; what they have to
> do is repent of their sins and turn to God, the fountain
> of all life. Either we repent or we perish. (153)

It is this *metanoia*, this repentance and conversion, that
the evangelistic socioeconomic challenge hopes to bring
about. The sinner is transformed, takes on a new identity,
and has a change of orientation. That person's life is "deci-
sively altered, reshaped, and turned around" (Wallis,
1976:20). It is a *metanoia* of which the Zacchaeus narrative
is a paradigm (Luke 19:1-10).

Zacchaeus shows that the proper response to the challenge of the reign of God involves a reorientation of our
values in line with those of God's reign. In his conversion,
greed and self-seeking were converted into generosity.
Dishonest dealing was countered by restitution. There was
a behavioral change. Salvation came to his house because
of this behavioral *metanoia* (Posterski: 24; Dyrness: 136).
This is exactly what is needed today when the evangelistic
challenge is made in the socioeconomic sphere.

Certainly the gospel is not reducible to the economic
sphere, whether in economic liberation or in the challenge
to the economic mighty. Nor does the church have economic or political competence, as Stransky rightly points
out. We cannot leap from eschatology to practical econom-

ics and politics with ready-made evangelical solutions which ignore social ethics and the achievement of civil liberties. But the church must be concerned for the evangelization of people when people are "counter-educated" by selfish political, economic, and social structures. The church then must speak out and act; otherwise the church will be "counter-evangelizing" (Stransky: 348).

The social evangelistic challenge to the contemporary North American person can't be limited to the area of economics and material possessions. There are many other aspects of life which are just as oppressive to marginal persons, such as racism, ageism, and sexism, particularly masculine sexism. These along with capitalism, Jürgen Moltmann and Douglas Meeks label as expressions of North America's neopaganism (cited in Krass: 146-151).

Some fundamentalists forcefully challenge creeping secularism and secular humanism in society as neopagan; with equal force, we must confront the evils of racism and sexism wherever they raise an ugly head.

> Where the facts of race, class, and sex are used to oppress and divide, the gospel message must speak of the meaning of the cross and resurrection of Christ in abolishing former divisions and barriers and creating a new humanity where all men and women are reconciled as one. . . . The preaching of the gospel in our times, as in other times, must involve the call to "repent, for the kingdom of heaven is at hand."
>
> (Wallis, 1976:22)

This *metanoia* which must take place has to involve equality, peoplehood of brothers and sisters in Christ, justice, reconciliation, and forgiveness. Without this, we cannot enter into the reign of God.

The evangelistic task and the reign of God should not

be limited to the human, internal, personal sphere. We need to recognize that issues such as ecology and our attitude to the environment are important areas to be addressed in the evangelistic enterprise (Roxburgh). Our surroundings and our environment are part of God's created order and therefore are included in his reign. Our attitude to God's creation speaks loudly about our attitude to God. The evangelist is challenged to confront the destroyers of the environment in the same manner as the rapers of humans are confronted.

No matter what the issues may be—social, personal, physical, or religious—God calls us to engage them in the evangelistic task. Yet in my own denomination, many would argue that our evangelistic task is limited to the three angels' message of Revelation 14:6-12. They proclaim that the hour of God's judgment has come, a judgment which in this interpretation is heavenly without an earthly component. Thus believers are to follow the example of the three angels and have no business getting involved in challenging the social issues in society.

However, in a recent editorial in the church's main paper, Roy Adams took on that point of view and disposed of it. He argued that there is no conflict between proclamation of the three angels' messages (of Rev. 14) and engagement with contemporary issues and concern. When these messages are correctly understood and comprehended, we recognize that they are not in opposition to social action in the world.

We can't truly "fear God and give him glory" (14:7) without "confronting the arrogant sacrilege that permeates contemporary society—in the arts, in entertainment, in our social mores." We can't "worship him who made heaven and earth, the sea and the springs of water" (14:7), "with nary a concern for the willful and criminal pollution and destruction of the environment" (Adams: 5).

Adams goes on to say that

> people cannot effectively "worship Him" while under
> the tyranny of oppression and bondage. That's why
> God's message through Moses to Pharaoh was *"Let
> my people go,* so that they may worship me" (Exod.
> 7:16, NIV). God's people today cannot credibly sum-
> mon the world to worship the Creator and at the same
> time have no concern for freedom and liberation. We
> cannot proclaim "the hour of his judgment has come"
> and have no concern for equity and justice in the
> world (Rev. 14:7, NIV). (Adams: 5)

As noted earlier, for Adams it is clear that believers
can't be "heavenly minded zombies" totally detached from
the social realities of contemporary society. We must be
engaged in the issues and concerns of the society which af-
fect the total person.

He goes further to emphasize that the three angels'
message (Rev. 14) expresses God's concern for the total
person, not just for the spiritual dimension. Although salvation has an individual and personal dimension, "the
apocalyptic nature of the book of Revelation should alert
us to the fact that its concern and issues go beyond the individual to the corporate structures of the world, spiritual
and secular" (Adams: 5).

My paradigm for evangelism here is not the book of
Revelation. Yet like that book, Luke certainly recognizes
the cosmic and the non-material dimensions of the battle
between the forces of evil and the forces of good. Contemporary evangelism needs to find creative ways to challenge those forces.

Church-growth practitioners like Peter Wagner have
recognized that challenging supernatural forces which
war against the reign of God is an important component of

the evangelistic task (Wagner: 97-98). It is not important whether we go as far as Wagner and his colleague Chuck Kraft go. What is more important is that we do not ignore any of the forces of evil: spiritual, social, political, personal. All must be confronted; all must be challenged in the name of Christ.

Contextual and Incarnational

I have grounded this work in the hermeneutical pre-supposition that the theology and missiology of Luke is uniquely contextual. Evangelism today must also be contextual and incarnational; it must be relevant and lived.

A Relevant Approach

Luke, like the rest of the Synoptic writers and all the New Testament authors, were task-oriented theologians. Their theology grew out of their mission in their particular context. They theologized to deal with their particular situation. Luke, then, was one of four attempts at contextualizing the Gospel for different situations and contexts (Bosch, 1991a:61).

One of the major discoveries over prior decades is that all theological reflection is contextual—whether it be by biblically inspired authors or by subsequent authors who reflect on the Scriptures. But only in recent years has there been an increasingly overt emphasis on contextualization in theological and missiological thinking (Conn, 1993:96). Missiologists have now realized that evangelism must be contextually appropriate to the people and the time in which they live.

The presentation and presence of the gospel, the good news of the reign of God, is never given, lived, and experienced in a vacuum. It has to be presented and experienced in terms that make sense to the receiving community. "Authentic evangelism must be forged in the praxis of taking the gospel to ordinary men and women, and thereby having to find the appropriate form and method for its presentation" (Watson, 1985:219; see Green: 115).

Among the many fears which should haunt contemporary evangelists is the fear of being irrelevant and out of touch. Out of their faithfulness to the gospel, they are called to connect with the needs and demands of today's world (Castro: 17). Any evangelists worth their salt know that people respond wholeheartedly to the gospel when they realize that it is relevant to their particular needs (Oosterwal: 59-60). Evangelists must, therefore, take careful note of the context of those being evangelized. They must study the social and personal circumstances of their existence to make sure the gospel as proclaimed will be relevant.

We need to be careful in the use of uniform programs, techniques, and strategies handed down from denominational headquarters, coming out of the "sales department" (Pippert: 13). I am not totally devaluing such programs. Standard programs have their value and have some strengths. But evangelism in a pluralistic and differentiated society like North America has to move beyond generalized and generic pragmatic strategies. It needs to be "multidimensional and highly pluriform" (Oosterwal: 59).

"The mission strategy for each congregation must increasingly be shaped by the values, needs, and style of its context. In pluralistic cultures, there are a wide variety of values which can change from neighborhood to neighborhood" (Roxburgh: 65). Thus an evangelistic strategy which is effective in one neighborhood, culture, or context may be quite ineffective in another.

Too often we treat evangelism as an abstract activity which can be standardized worldwide. We fail to take into consideration the nature of the modern city versus the rural community. We fail to come to terms with cultural and linguistic situations, as well as philosophical and ideological outlooks.

For example, in Jamaica—a communal society with strong African roots—a more traditional door-to-door approach with in-home Bible study is far more effective than in the U.S. Northwest. The Northwest fosters a frontier, individualist worldview. In Jamaica, a society poorer in material ways, it is acceptable and effective to have a direct-assistance program for initiates into the reign of God. In the Northwest, however, one's privacy is highly valued. This difference shows how inadequate it would be to create a monolithic strategy of wholistic evangelism and apply the same in both rural Jamaica and urban Seattle.

Because we fail to contextualize our evangelism, members of the body of Christ do not treat it as a normal part of their existence. Becky Pippert tells a personal story which illustrates this point. She asked a girl if she felt comfortable about evangelism. The girl replied: "Oh yes, I do it twice a week" (30). Pippert comments that evangelism is not something one "does" and then gets back to normal living. It involves "taking people seriously, getting across to their island of concerns and needs, and then sharing Christ as Lord in the context of our natural living situations" (30).

The reality, however, is that the majority of Christians in North America (and especially in the Northwest) find the traditional approaches to evangelism uncomfortable and even repelling. Yet a survey found that 72 percent of mainline pastors and 86 percent of evangelical clergy placed evangelism in North America as their number-one priority (Van Engen, 1992:25).

Van Engen therefore raises questions: If evangelism is given such a high priority, why are churches doing so poorly in this area? Why do churches decline? Why is there "negative growth"? There have been numerous evangelistic approaches over recent decades, with little success. We have been concerned with "how" to do evangelism and forgotten the most important part of the process—"the hearers" (1992:25-26). We have failed to reckon with the contextual felt needs of the ones to be evangelized.

Yet many people want evangelism to be simply "the old, old story." That story "was good for Paul and Silas, and it's good enough for me." But as Walter Hollenweger declares, the good news is an event, something new, not just "a repetition of something. . . . It demands rethinking and reshaping instant by instant" (cited by Krass: 104).

Yes, old evangelistic strategies for the most part no longer work. Christianity as normally presented is not making sense in our culture. The evangelism which Luke outlines in narrative form was tailored to his culture and setting. It was not simply propositional; it was contextual. So we also must understand our culture and tailor our evangelistic strategies to be contextually relevant.

This is a call to reinvent evangelism (Posterski: 14-15). It is a call to go beyond words. It is a call to reread the signs in our varied and unique cultural and social settings, to meet people where they are, where their felt needs are.

All credible studies confirm that North America is becoming more and more a secular society. The gospel of Jesus Christ as traditionally presented is making less and less sense. It is our contention that if effective contact is to be made in such a society, it has to be made at the level of discerned needs. "A need is felt," says Jon Paulien, "whenever life does not fully meet a person's expectation" (36). A secular society is far more pluralistic than a traditional religious one. Therefore, needs perceived in a secular society will be more diverse.

The strategies for presenting the whole gospel in the North American context has to be varied in order to be effective. Public types of evangelism, especially "event evangelism," are helpful in some contexts where recognized needs are similar. This is true in two-thirds-world societies like Jamaica. But the U.S. Northwest is much less monolithic than Jamaica. There is a broad cross-section of poor yet religious people in Jamaica; in the U.S. Northwest, the larger cross-section is middle class, secular individualist.

Hence, public evangelism (social and religious) would be more successful in reaching felt needs in Jamaica than in the Northwest. A multiplicity of strategies would need to be developed contextually for cities like Seattle and Walla Walla, with less emphasis on "event" evangelism.

The church in North America has given some creative responses to the challenge of secularization. Thus the Adventist "Caring Church" concept shows the church's openness to the needs of the world. Yet there is still a strong emphasis on public and "event" evangelism in all segments of the society.[8] A famous and successful international evangelist himself noted that public evangelism as traditionally and presently conducted does not reach the secular mind (Cox: 77).

Church members have little contact and few ties with secular people. This leads Evangelist Cox to state,

> Being able to communicate the Word of God effectively requires that we become acquainted with these people personally. Christ met the people where they were. He lived among them, worked with them in the carpenter's shop, and talked to them in the streets and on the hillside. He attended their weddings and ate with known sinners.
>
> Because of our tendency to isolate ourselves, we are out of touch with "the man on the street." We live in our small communities and around our institutions; we talk to one another, and our dealings are usually

with one another; and we have basically cut ourselves off from the very thing we have been called to do. (79)

Over a century ago, Ellen White, who helped guide the formation of the Adventist church, argued this basic point. We "must learn to adapt our labors to the conditions of people—to meet [them] where they are" (57). "We are to study the fields carefully and are not to think that we must follow the same methods in every place" (125).

The U.S. Northwest is highly urbanized in addition to being secularized; this adds to the demand for diverse evangelistic strategies. Carlos Schwantes, a Northwest historian, notes a tendency for people to cluster in a few urban areas. For example, there are 597 persons per square mile in the State of Washington's King County, which includes the region's largest city, Seattle, with half a million residents. On the other hand, some counties in eastern Washington have less than six persons per square mile. And there are counties in central Idaho and eastern Oregon which are even more lightly populated (4).

As the Northwest becomes more urbanized, an urban contextual approach needs to be taken. Furthermore, "urbanism's integrating nature will demand we look again at the relationship between evangelism and social transformation" (Conn, 1993:101). We need to examine urbanism in general and also in particular, assessing the unique social and religious idiosyncrasies of Northwest cities.

The Northwest is only one example.[9] The challenges faced here are in varying degrees similar to those in the industrialized Western world. The present status-quo Christian church is becoming more and more irrelevant in our sophisticated society. If we are to become relevant, we must listen to what society is saying and read the signs of the times to see where it is going; and we need to read the Scripture and proclaim Christ's gospel for the present day.

This will mean recapturing the wholistic evangelistic strategy laid out by Luke. The ministry of John, Jesus, and the early church is a credible paradigm for modern society. The modern evangelist is called to demonstrate such living as well as proclamation. Evangelism must

> be grounded in a *credible demonstration* that life lived by the pattern of commitment to Jesus is imaginable, possible, and relevant in the modern and postmodern age. This requires more than . . . verbal witness to rest on consistent living. That tended to mean living exemplary, moral lives as upstanding citizens. The requirements of moral faithfulness are no less now, but more importantly the current need is for a demonstration that faith in the gospel of God can be the genuine organizing center integrating the fragmented pieces of modern living. Only when it is seen lived out by someone who believes that way will the message about the reign of God have credibility. (Hunsberger: 404-405)

A Lived Approach

I will end this work with some stories of churches which have incarnated themselves, following the Lukan paradigm of wholistic evangelism—personal as well as social. Like Luke-Acts, there is a strong social component because that is most contextually relevant for their situation and calling. Tom Sine gives us the first four. The first three are from the Northwest.

A suburban church in Portland, Oregon, broke down the congregation into small groups, creating organic networks. These groups are involved both in personal and social mission outreach. Nuclear families, single-parent families, senior and divorced persons—all find a fulfilling level of commitment. Over 50 percent of these are actively involved in mission outside the church (Sine: 46). They not only find hope but they give hope.

There is a house church in Seattle composed of twenty-two persons (including sixteen adults). Besides being involved in individual ministries, their mission finds them cleaning yards and painting houses for seniors who are unable to perform this upkeep for themselves. Sixty percent of their funds are invested in mission outside their fellowship. They are involved in peace-and-justice efforts in the Seattle area. They are a countercultural presence of the reign of God in Seattle (Sine: 44-45).

The University Baptist Church in Seattle overwhelmingly voted to use its church building as a sanctuary for undocumented refugees from El Salvador. This action, says Sine, "brought about a remarkable revitalization of congregational life as numbers put themselves on the line for their growing family of those who have escaped torture, persecution, and death in El Salvador (13-14).

A church in Plain City, Ohio, sent seven of its members to Haiti to be involved in construction, agriculture, and handicraft for two years (Sine: 13).

Alan Roxburgh relates the story of Danforth Baptist church in downtown Toronto. It is a story of how a new generation reflected the values of their parents (who left a decaying changing neighborhood). They moved back into the city and engaged in a successful wholistic church growth and evangelism outreach. I quote at length from his own story:

> Growth came through such things as dynamic worship, contemporary music and praise, nurture and mission groups, outreach ministries, team leadership, and an openness to all that the Spirit wanted to give and say to us through one another. One outreach ministry, called Danforth Café, was designed to pre-

sent contemporary themes and issues in an informal, nonthreatening atmosphere where people could discuss faith and values. Through the café we touched non-Christians from both the neighborhood and the larger city. Operating biweekly, this ministry addressed issues such as refugee needs, sexual abuse, housing, the environment, spirituality, and values. Excellent music and other arts were a major component in its life. . . .

In cooperation with a government agency, we initiated a housing project for economically disadvantaged single adults. Four large rehabbed houses were opened to about eight residents each. A member of the residents eventually joined our cell groups and became active in the church as a result of the friendships and care they received from Christians. Danforth also developed a counseling ministry that not only responded to needs in the congregation but also served the neighborhood. (Roxburgh: 18-19)

Many growing churches in one way or another are engaging in a more wholistic approach to ministry and evangelism. In the second section of *Evangelism and Social Involvement*, Delos Miles narrates numerous stories of wholistic mission enterprise by individuals, churches, and parachurch organizations.

Evangelism needs to be reinvented and actually recaptured for our Western society. Buying more prime-time television, handing out colored tracts, and putting on a showy evangelistic event—these are scratching where most North Americans are not itching. To be effective in our contemporary society, we need to be doing and experiencing the kind of prophetic, complete, and wholistic evangelism modeled by the churches and Christian communities mentioned above.

CONCLUSION

Western Christianity has divided what was initially inseparable. Jesus Christ never meant the evangelistic task to be only an inner personal matter without a social component. The powerfully persuasive influence of Greek dualism has infected Western civilization and influenced our theology and missiology. It undergirds a heresy that appears to be orthodox, that there are two worlds: the private and the public, the spiritual and the social. Thus the evangelistic and spiritual task has been limited to the private world, and the social is relegated to the secular nonsalvific world. What God had joined together, human beings have put asunder.

This was not always the case. True reform movements throughout the Christian era have recognized that there is an intimate connection between the social and spiritual aspects of Christian outreach. During the early part of the twentieth century, with the fundamentalist-modernist debate, the rigid separation was institutionalized to a larger degree than previously. As we enter the twenty-first century, there is a growing cry to recapture what was lost in the religio-political wars. There is a call for us to seek strong biblical roots for this renewed worldview.

We have found a strong paradigm in the two-volume work of Luke. Hermeneutically, we have argued, it is possible to see different perspectives in different biblical books. Biblical authors wrote out of their unique contexts. We must be careful not to make any one document or particular text to be *the* norm for theological or missiological praxis. We find it, therefore, unfortunate that Matthew's great commission should serve as the only ground of operation for evangelism. Matthew's commission is valid, especially when we follow "all things" that Christ "commanded." But Luke also presents a paradigm which should not be ignored. His theological and missiological reflections, via the medium of narrative, present us with a wholistic view of mission from which we can extrapolate for our times.

We have learned about the wholistic and prophetic evangelistic teaching and practice of John the Baptist, Jesus, and the early church. Luke focused strongly on the social component without ignoring the personal or the role of the Holy Spirit in the entire enterprise. The Holy Spirit rested upon Jesus and anointed him to reach the poor, the sick, the marginal, and the outcasts (Luke 4:18-19).

Likewise, the Holy Spirit or the Spirit of Jesus empowered and led the church in all its ministries of being Christ's witnesses (Luke 24:47-49; Acts 1:8). This included overcoming discrimination in their midst (Acts 15:7-11, 28-29) and rescuing those sick, hungry, or oppressed by evil spirits (Acts 3:6; 6:3; 16:18). The evangelistic mission in Luke-Acts included the giving of hope to those on the margins. It was an invitation to the reign of God and an initiation into that reign.

But the evangelistic task brought conflict, for it had a confrontational dimension. Those on the side of the mighty and powerful, those implicitly or explicitly opposing the reign of God, or those whom Christ was anoint-

ed to reach—all were challenged to repent and be converted. The *metanoia* had to be spiritual as well as social, because for Luke, sins were spiritual as well as social.

To evangelize faithfully in today's world, we need to
recapture the paradigm presented by Luke, and engage it
in new and contemporary ways for each unique situation.
Only thus can we be successful when measured by the
standards of the gospel of Jesus Christ.

We need to proclaim hope to the socially marginalized
of our time, letting them know that the reign of God is not
only future, but present too. It is already here, though it is
not yet completely fulfilled. It is now, and it is hereafter.
The contemporary oppressed and marginalized include
women, ethnic minorities, the poor, and those suffering
family estrangements. They all need the good news of Jesus Christ in both spiritual as well as social terms. They
need that fresh word from Jesus in our time: *"Today* this
scripture has been fulfilled in your hearing" (Luke 4:21).

Like Jesus, our evangelistic task must simultaneously
challenge the social and spiritual structures as well as persons which are opposed to the reign of God. In the same
manner that we vigorously announce the good news of
hope, we must equally denounce all sins, injustices, and
evil works of powers and principalities.

As we seek to reflect Jesus in our mission, our
wholistic evangelism and evangelization will be humanizing and liberating, and at the same time challenging and
confrontive. It must invite persons into the reign of God
on earth and create an atmosphere for that reign, so that
we can say, "Today salvation has come" (Luke 19:9). Thus
we prepare for the final glorious consummation, when
God's will is done on earth as fully as it is in heaven.

Notes

Chapter 1. Historical Overview

1. The Great Awakenings are approximately dated as follows: the first, 1726-1750s; the second, 1790s-1850s; the third (by analogy), 1875-1914.

2. J. Verkuyl notes that the social-gospel movement arose also in reaction to "the exclusive emphasis of some on individual conversion and of others on the [church-centered style] found in much of traditional home and foreign missions" (194).

3. For a good bibliography, see Patterson, 76, note 7.

4. This relates to the struggle to interpret Revelation 20.

Premillennialists believe things will worsen and then Christ's return will bring in a thousand years of messianic rule; there is debate over whether Christ's return to rescue the saints (the "rapture" of 1 Thess. 4:13-18) will be before or after a period of intense tribulation.

Postmillennialists believe that this present church age is the millennium, when Satan is being bound and overcome in church and society (Luke 10:18; 11:14-23; Mark 3:23-27), and that afterward Christ will return.

Amillennialists believe that Revelation 20 is to be understood symbolically rather than literally, representing the perfection of the martyrs' reign with Christ—or of Christ's triumph over Satan in the church.

5. See Patterson, 86-91, for more on the universalist stance of the report (and of Ernest Hockins, the mind behind the report) in relation to other religions. According to some historians, this led to missions being reduced to social compassion.

Chapter 2. Hermeneutical Method

1. I'm indebted to George Rice, 33ff., for much of this summary illustration.

2. See Van Engen, 1993b:32-35, for his delineation of how to approach the Bible as an interwoven tapestry of God's action in history, of missional themes and motifs in context.

Chapter 3. Reading Luke-Acts Again

1. Regarding the stem *euangeli-*, the verb form is used ten times in Luke, once in Matthew, never in Mark or John, 16 times in Acts, and 27 times in the epistles, and twice in Revelation. The noun *good news* is used four times in Matthew, eight times in Mark (if counting 16:15), never in Luke or John, twice in Acts, 60 times in the epistles, and once in Revelation. *Evangelists* are mentioned once in Acts and twice in the epistles.

2. Little attention is given to the emphasis in the last part of the great commission on the comprehensive task of "teaching them to obey everything" Jesus commanded, as in chapters 5-8, 10, 25, etc., in Matthew.

3. *Euangelizō* occurs 11 times in Luke and Matthew, 16 times in Acts, and 29 times in other New Testament books. However, Barrett spends three paragraphs on Luke and Matthew, three on the rest of the New Testament (other than Acts), but 15 paragraphs on Acts, arguing that it is the major and most typical (12-14). But we may ask, Is Acts most typical? Or is it the case that *as interpreted*, Acts fits a certain evangelical ideology? We agree that Acts provides a major and important understanding. But it is no more important than other usages.

4. See particularly Barr, 206-262, for his critique of Kittel's *Theological Dictionary (TWNT/TDNT)*.

5. See George Rice, 45ff., for an extended discussion on this. On 55ff. he suggests that the deliverance could also be extended to the release from cultic traditions.

6. Compare Luke 7:22 for Jesus' healing activity in response to John the Baptist's query as to whether he was the one to come.

7. See Tannehill, 1986:68, for the possibility that "the year of the Lord's favor" is synonymous with the reign of God.

8. The poor here are definitely not a spiritual category, but a literal socioeconomic one. It is significant that Luke does not have the phrase "in spirit" as found in Matthew 5:3. In my book *Poverty and Wealth in James* (1987:33-34), I argue that not even in Matthew should the term be taken primarily as a spiritual concept. Matthew parallels the

pattern of the Mosaic Law and Qumran by making reference to the economic poor in the spiritual community.

9. Messianic Rule, 1QSa 2.3-10; Damascus Rule, CD 15.15-17. Cf. Deut. 23:1; Lev. 21:18; 2 Sam. 5:8; Matt. 21:14.

10. See Bosch, 1989:13, note 18, for a contrary opinion. This above position is an adjustment to my earlier wholesale rejection of Jeremias's contention that the poor include the hungry, those who weep, are sick; the last, the lost, the sinner, etc. (Jeremias: 113). Although I still think Jeremias's definition for poor in the Synoptics is too broad, it seems to me that in contexts like these being discussed, "sinners" is to be interpreted socially (see Maynard-Reid, 1987:32-34).

11. The emphasis of these parables is not so much on that which was lost but on the finder, the searcher for the lost. The shepherd, the woman, and the father are the figures of importance. They are the ones who bring the lost into the reign of God.

12. Much of the data in this section is based on Tannehill's commentary, 1986:134-139; cf. Sider: 66-67.

13. Bosch, 1991:103, notes that Luke should really be called "the evangelist of the rich" rather than an evangelist of the poor. However, we are arguing that it is not an either-or situation, but a both-and program. When evangelism is seen as *hope* and *challenge*, the unreconciled dichotomy becomes a mute point.

14. See my 1981 Th.D. dissertation for an extensive description of the economic world of Palestine in the first century, showing how the rich oppressed the poor.

15. Cassidy states that "by holding on to more possessions than he needed, he proved himself a fool in the sight of God" (25-26). But the text in reality doesn't speak about "more possessions than needed." Its context is abundance of possession. Cassidy waters down Luke's impact when he tends to add the word "surplus" to "possessions" (25-33).

16. At another time Jesus challenged the disciples to live simply. When he sent them out to preach the reign of God, he told them to take nothing for their journey—not even staff, bag, money, or a spare tunic (9:3). Similarly, the Seventy are instructed to take no purse, bag, or sandals (10:4; Cassidy: 26).

17. The Greek word used here for "distribute" occurs only four times in the New Testament; three times in Luke-Acts, two of which are found in Acts 2:45 and 4:35; Tannehill, 1990:46, note 8.

Chapter 4. Theological Motifs in Luke-Acts

1. See George Rice, 105-106, who argues for an internal, personal, spiritual translation.

2. See note 9 for chapter 3, above.

3. For examples of other texts where healing accompanies the proclamation of the good news by the apostles, see Acts 5:15-16; 8:5-7; 9:33-34; 14:8-11; 19:11-12.

4. We already suggested that the "captives" in Luke 4:18 could be the economically oppressed poor who were enslaved by debt and/or in debtors' prison.

5. In Luke's Gospel the word *hamartōlos*, sinner, is used more often (17 times) than in Matthew (five) and Mark (six). Cf. Bosch, 1991:105-106.

6. Used ten times in Luke-Acts, and only seven times elsewhere in the New Testament.

7. John R. W. Stott argues that the punctiliar event should be categorized as regeneration—the instantaneous and complete work of God. He regards conversion, however, to be more a process than an event. Thus he makes a clear distinction between the punctiliar regeneration and the linear conversion. Nevertheless, he points out that "no doubt in the experience of many there is a point at which the turn called conversion becomes complete and dawning faith becomes saving faith. But even then, the converted Christian's saving faith work is far from done. Conversion is only the beginning" (116).

8. See Luke 3:3, 8; 5:32; 15:7; 24:47; Acts 3:31; 11:18; 13:24; 19:4; 20:21; 26:20.

9. Schniewind notes that conversion in the Hebrew Scriptures is turning back to God; the prophets constantly speak of turning from idols to the worship of Yahweh. In turning to God, the faithful were promised a new age when God's new order rules over them and they would receive a new heart. "A new self will be created, God will take away the heart of stone and give us a heart of flesh" (268-269).

However, this presentation of personal piety and of the prophets is not consistent with those ancient spokesmen. For the most part, the prophets spoke in the same mode as did John the Baptist. Thus Philip Potter is correct when he notes that *turning to God* in the Hebrew Scriptures "is not merely a matter of individual reorientation. It has personal and corporate dimensions" (313).

10. I'm indebted to Van Engen's class syllabus, 1993a:20-21, for many of these references. Though his basic focus is on Acts, see his entire syllabus for the Holy Spirit and mission in Luke-Acts.

Chapter 5. Missiological Implications

1. Other New Testament models are also wholistic, but they are beyond the scope of this study. For example, see Matt. 5:9, 13-15, 38-48; 25:31-46; Rom. 12:1-2, 13-21; Gal. 6:1-10; James 2:14-26.

2. Sine, however, notes that "ironically, some Christians are able to believe at one and the same time in two very different views of the future: the first in which they pessimistically believe everything is inevitably going to get worse and worse and the destruction of the planet earth is at hand; and the second in which they optimistically believe the American economy is going to grow 4 percent every year and they are going to enjoy ever more consumptive lifestyles. To illustrate the extent of this dualism, someone has reported that an author of prophetic books that predict the world is going to end tomorrow has invested the profits from those books in long-term American growth bonds!" (29).

3. We are aware of the debate regarding the distinction and similarities between "mission" and "evangelism." We will not argue those points here (see Bosch, 1987:98-99). We feel that the argument stands whether one treats them as identical or separate.

4. See Abraham, 44ff., for a detailed description of the case for and against evangelism as proclamation.

5. Of course, on the other hand Watson notes that there are those who "seek for the fullness of the New Age through the endeavors of worldly involvement, by implication continuing the promise of eternal life to an ephemeral existence" (1983:6).

6. Although our emphasis in this study is on the social dimension of evangelism, we must constantly be reminded about the salvific importance of personal faith in the economy of salvation; and the role of the incarnate Jesus in it. The foremost proponent of the social gospel at the turn of the century, Walter Rauschenbusch, argued that the social and political component of mission does not bring salvation.

"Salvation came by the coming of the Son of God into humanity, initiating the new humanity with a force not previously among us. It came by the coming of the spirit of the risen Christ, transforming individuals, pressing them into a new society, inspiring new thoughts, impelling to new undertakings, making all things new" (272).

7. In chapter 10 of his book, Delos Miles discusses this at length (145-154). He outlines a radical call with which he has some problems now, but he feels prophetic evangelism may pick up momentum as we move into the next century (148-150).

8. For a collection of articles which address the issue on which the title is based, see *Meeting the Secular Mind: Some Adventist Perspectives*, by Rasi and Guy.

John Brunt, a theologian and biblical scholar at Walla Walla College School of Theology in the Northwest, wrote one of the most recent missionary and evangelistic books for the Adventist church. In it he attempts to make SDA teachings relevant to a contemporary audience. But the focus of the work is on the personal level, not social or public. Brunt, being a Pauline scholar, writes out of the context of the traditionally formulated Pauline model of evangelism. I'm convinced that the Lukan wholistic model explained above is more relevant for pluralistic secular society today.

9. William Pannell notes that according to the 1980 census figures, 75 percent of all Americans now live in cities. This census reveals a global reality: the world has gone urban. More people are living in cities today than the total world population 150 years ago. Pannell also notes that churches have neglected the cities. Evangelistic crusades are not held inside the cities but on the fringes, and they are really catering to people who already are Christians (9-10). Thus our philosophy, methods, and strategies of evangelism are not geared to meet the needs perceived by the population of urban centers.

Bibliography

Abraham, William J.
  1989   *The Logic of Evangelism.* Grand Rapids: Eerdmans.
Adams, Roy
  1994   "As We Wait-3." *Adventist Review* 171.23:5.
Arias, Mortimer
  1984   *Announcing the Reign of God: Evangelization and the Sub-versive Memory of Jesus.* Philadelphia: Fortress.
Barr, James
  1961   *The Semantics of Biblical Language.* Great Britain: Oxford University.
Barrett, David
  1987   *Evangelize! A Historical Survey of the Concept.* Birmingham, Ala.: New Hope.
Birch, Bruce C., and Larry L. Rasmussen
  1989   *Bible and Ethics in the Christian Life.* Rev. and expanded ed. Minneapolis: Augsburg.
Boff, Leonardo
  1991   *New Evangelization: Good News to the Poor.* Maryknoll, N.Y.: Orbis.
Bosch, David J.
  1983   "Evangelism and Social Transformation." In *The Church in Response to Human Need,* ed. Tom Sine, 273-292. Monrovia, Calif.: MARC.

1987 "Evangelism: Theological Currents and Cross-Currents Today." *International Bulletin of Missionary Research* 11:98-103.

1989 "Mission in Jesus' Way: A Perspective from Luke's Gospel." *Missionalia* 1 (Apr.): 3-21.

1991a *Transforming Mission: Paradigm Shifts in Theology of Mission.* Maryknoll, N.Y.: Orbis.

1991b "Toward a New Paradigm of Mission." In *Mission in the 1990s,* ed. Gerald Anderson, James Phillips, and Robert Coote, 60-64. Grand Rapids: Eerdmans.

Brueggemann, Walter

1993 *Biblical Perspectives on Evangelism: Living in a Three-Storied Universe.* Nashville: Abingdon.

Brunt, John C.

1993 *Good News for Troubled Times.* Hagerstown, Md.: Review and Herald.

Cassidy, Richard J.

1978 *Jesus, Politics, and Society: A Study of Luke's Gospel.* Maryknoll, N.Y.: Orbis.

Castro, Emilio

1985 *Sent Free: Mission and Unity in Perspective of the Kingdom.* Grand Rapids: Eerdmans.

Conn, Harvie M.

1982 *Evangelism. Doing Justice and Preaching Grace.* Grand Rapids: Zondervan.

1993 "A Contextual Theology of Mission for the City." In *The Good News of the Kingdom: Mission Theology for the Third Millennium,* ed. Charles Van Engen, Dean Gilliland, and Paul Pierson, 96-105. Maryknoll, N.Y.: Orbis.

Conzelmann, Hans

1960 *The Theology of St. Luke.* London: Faber & Faber.

Costas, Orlando

1979 *The Integrity of Mission: The Inner Life and Outreach of the Church.* New York: Harper & Row.

Cox, Kenneth O.

1987 "Evangelistic Problems and Suggestions." In *Meeting*

the Secular Mind: Some Adventist Perspectives, ed. Humberto M. Rasi and Fritz Guy, 77-83. Berrien Springs, Mich.: Andrews University Press.

CRESR '82 Report
1983   "Evangelism and Social Responsibility." In *The Church in Response to Human Need*, ed. Tom Sine, 439-487. Monrovia, Calif.: MARC.

Dennis, James S.
1897   *Christian Missions and Social Progress*. 3 volumes. New York: Revell.

Dyrness, William
1983   *Let the Earth Rejoice: A Biblical Theology of Holistic Mission*. Pasadena: Fuller Seminary Press.

Escobar, Samuel
1974   "Evangelism and Man's Search for Freedom, Justice and Fulfillment." In *Let the Earth Hear His Voice*, ed. J. D. Douglas, 303-326. Minneapolis: World Wide Publications.

Gaventa, Beverly Roberts
1982   " 'You Will Be My Witnesses': Aspects of Mission in the Acts of the Apostles." *Missiology: An International Review* 10.4:413-425.

Green, Michael
1970   *Evangelism in the Early Church*. Grand Rapids: Eerdmans.
1982   *Evangelism—Now and Then*. Downers Grove: Inter-Varsity.

Greenwalt, Glen
1994   "The Inspiration and Authority of Scripture." Unpublished manuscript. College Place, Wash.: Walla Walla College.

Henry, Carl F. H.
1947   *The Uneasy Conscience of Modern Fundamentalism*. Grand Rapids: Eerdmans.

Hoekendijk, J. C.
1966   *The Church Inside Out*. Philadelphia: Westminster.

Hunsberger, George R.
1991 "The Newbigin Gauntlet: Developing a Domestic Missiology for North America." *Missiology: An International Review* 19.4:391-408.

Jeremias, Joachim
1971 *New Testament Theology: The Proclamation of Jesus.* New York: Charles Scribner's Sons.

Keck, Leander E., and J. Louis Martyn, eds.
1980 *Studies in Luke-Acts.* Philadelphia: Fortress Press.

Krass, Alfred
1982 *Evangelizing Neopagan North America: The Word That Frees.* Scottdale, Pa.: Herald Press.

Kuhn, Thomas
1970 *The Structure of Scientific Revolutions.* Chicago: Univ. of Chicago Press.

Ladd, George Eldon
1964 *Jesus and the Kingdom: The Eschatology of Biblical Realism.* New York: Harper & Row.

Linden, Ingemar
1978 *The Last Trump: An Historico-Genetical Study of Some Important Chapters in the Making and Development of the Seventh-Day Adventist Church.* Frankfurt: Peter Lang.

Linder, Robert
1977 "The Resurgence of Evangelical Social Concern." In *The Evangelicals: What They Believe, Who They Are, Where They Are Changing,* ed. David F. Wells and John D. Woodbridge, 209-230. Rev. ed. Grand Rapids: Baker.

Marsden, George M.
1977 "From Fundamentalism to Evangelicalism: A Historical Analysis." In *The Evangelicals: What They Believe, Who They Are, Where They are Changing,* ed. David F. Wells and John D. Woodbridge, 142-162. Rev. ed. Grand Rapids: Baker.

Maynard-Reid, Pedrito U.
1981 "Poor and Rich in the Epistle of James: A Socio-Historical and Exegetical Study." Th.D. dissertation, Andrews University.

1987   *Poverty and Wealth in James.* Maryknoll, N.Y.: Orbis.

1990   "Called to Share." In *The Midas Trap,* ed. David Neff, 65-70. Wheaton, Ill.: Christianity Today.

McGavran, Donald A.

1990   *Understanding Church Growth.* Grand Rapids: Eerdmans.

Miles, Delos

1986   *Evangelism and Social Involvement.* Nashville: Broadman.

Motte, Mary

1991   "The Poor: Starting Point for Mission." In *Mission in the 1990s,* ed. Gerald Anderson, James Phillips, and Robert Coote, 50-54. Grand Rapids: Eerdmans.

Mouw, Richard J.

1973   *Political Evangelism.* Grand Rapids: Eerdmans.

Newbigin, Lesslie

1982   "Cross-Currents in Ecumenical and Evangelical Understanding of Mission." *International Bulletin of Missionary Research* 6.4:146-149.

1986   *Foolishness to the Greeks: The Gospel and Western Culture.* Grand Rapids: Eerdmans.

Oosterwal, Gottfried

1987   "The Process of Secularization." In *Meeting the Secular Mind: Some Adventist Perspectives,* ed. Humberto M. Rasi and Fritz Guy, 42-62. Berrien Springs, Mich.: Andrews University Press.

Pannell, William

1992   *Evangelism from the Bottom Up.* Grand Rapids: Zondervan.

Patterson, James Alan

1990   "The Loss of a Protestant Missionary Consensus: Foreign Missions and the Fundamentalist-Modernist Conflict." In *Earthen Vessels,* ed. Joel A. Carpenter and Wilbert R. Shenk, 73-91. Grand Rapids: Eerdmans.

Paulien, Jon K.

1987   "The Gospel in a Secular World." In *Meeting the Secular Mind: Some Adventist Perspectives,* ed. Humberto M. Rasi and Fritz Guy, 25-41. Berrien Springs, Mich.: Andrews University Press.

Perrin, Norman
1969 *What Is Redaction Criticism?* Philadelphia: Fortress.

Peters, George W.
1972 *A Biblical Theology of Missions.* Chicago: Moody.

Pierson, Paul E.
1989 "Missions and Community Development: A Historical Perspective." In *Christian Relief and Development: Developing Workers for Effective Ministry*, ed. Eddie Elliston, 7-22. Dallas: Word.

Pippert, Rebecca Manley
1979 *Out of the Salt Shaker and into the World: Evangelism as a Way of Life.* Downers Grove, Ill.: InterVarsity.

Pixley, G. V.
1981 *God's Kingdom: A Guide for Biblical Study.* Maryknoll, N.Y.: Orbis.

Posterski, Donald C.
1989 *Reinventing Evangelism: New Strategies for Presenting Christ in Today's World.* Downers Grove, Ill.: InterVarsity.

Potter, Philip
1968 "Evangelism and the World Council of Churches." *Ecumenical Review* 20.1:172-182.
1983 "Turning to Freedom and Fullness." *International Review of Missions* 72.287:313-323.

Rasi, Humberto M., and Fritz Guy, eds.
1987 *Meeting the Secular Mind: Some Adventist Perspectives.* Berrien Springs, Mich.: Andrews University Press.

Rauschenbusch, Walter
1966 "Conceptions of Mission." In *The Social Gospel in America, 1870-1966*, ed. Robert T. Handy, 268-273. New York: Oxford University Press.

Rice, George
1983 *Luke, A Plagiarist?* Mountain View, Calif.: Pacific Press.

Ro, Bong Rin
  1986   "The Perspectives of Church History from New Testament Times to 1960." In *In Word and Deed: Evangelism and Social Responsibility*, ed. Bruce J. Nichols, 11-40. Grand Rapids: Eerdmans.

Roxburgh, Alan J.
  1993   *Reaching a New Generation: Strategies for Tomorrow's Church*. Downers Grove, Ill.: InterVarsity.

Schniewind, Julius.
  1952   "The Biblical Doctrine of Conversion." *Scottish Journal of Theology* 5:267-281.

Schwantes, Carlos
  1989   *The Pacific Northwest: An Interpretive History*. Lincoln: University of Nebraska.

Scriven, Charles
  1988a "When the Jailhouse Rocks: In Defense of Evangelism for the Church of Today." *Spectrum* 18.3:22-28.
  1988b *The Transformation of Culture: Christian Social Ethics After H. Richard Niebuhr*. Scottdale, Pa.: Herald Press.

Senior, Donald, and Carroll Stuhlmueller
  1983   *The Biblical Foundations for Mission*. Maryknoll, N.Y.: Orbis.

Sider, Ronald J.
  1993   *One-Sided Christianity*. Grand Rapids: Zondervan.

Sine, Tom
  1985   *Taking Discipleship Seriously: A Radical Biblical Approach*. Valley Forge: Judson.

Smith, Linda
  1989   "Recent Historical Perspective of the Evangelical Tradition." In *Christian Relief and Development: Developing Workers for Effective Ministry*, ed. Edgar J. Elliston, 23-36. Dallas: Word.

Smith, Timothy
  1957   *Revivalism and Social Reform in Mid-Nineteenth-Century America*. New York: Abingdon.

Stott, John
  1975   *Christian Mission in the Modern World: What the Church Should Be Doing Now*. Downers Grove, Ill.: InterVarsity.

Stransky, Thomas F.
1982 "Evangelization, Missions, and Social Action: A Roman Catholic Perspective." *Review and Expositor* 79.2:343-350.

Strayer, Brian E.
1994 "William Miller's Helpers." *Adventist Review* 171.30:8-10.

Stromberg, Jean, compiler.
1983 *Mission and Evangelism: An Ecumenical Affirmation.* Geneva: World Council of Churches.

Tannehill, Robert C.
1986 *The Narrative Unity of Luke-Acts: A Literary Interpretation.* Vol. 1. Philadelphia: Fortress.
1990 *The Narrative Unity of Luke-Acts: A Literary Interpretation.* Vol. 2. Minneapolis: Fortress.

Tienou, Titi
1983 "Evangelism and Social Transformation." In *The Church in Response to Human Need,* ed. Tom Sine, 263-270. Monrovia, Calif.: MARC.

Van Engen, Charles
1990 "A Broadening Vision: Forty Years of Evangelical Theology of Mission, 1946-1986." In *Earthen Vessels,* ed. Joel A. Carpenter and Wilbert R. Shenk, 203-232. Grand Rapids: Eerdmans.
1992 *You Are My Witnesses.* New York: Reformed Church Press.
1993a Class syllabus, MT 523, "Holy Spirit and Mission in Luke-Acts." Pasadena: Fuller School of World Mission.
1993b "The Relation of Bible and Mission in Mission Theology." In *The Good News of the Kingdom: Mission Theology for the Third Millennium,* ed. Charles Van Engen, Dean Gilliland, and Paul Pierson, 27-36. Maryknoll, N.Y.: Orbis.

Verkuyl, J.
1978 *Contemporary Missiology: An Introduction.* Grand Rapids: Eerdmans.

Wagner, C. Peter
   1987   *Strategies for Church Growth: Tools for Effective Mission and Evangelism*. Ventura, Calif.: Regal.

Wallis, Jim
   1976   *Agenda for Biblical People*. New York: Harper & Row.
   1985   "The Rise of the Christian Conscience." *Sojourners* 14.1:12-16.

Watson, David Lowes
   1983   "Evangelism: A Disciplinary Approach." *International Bulletin of Missionary Research* 7.1:6-9.
   1985   "Prophetic Evangelism: The Good News of Global Grace." In *Wesleyan Theology Today: A Bicentennial Theological Consultation*, ed. Theodore Runyon, 219-226. Nashville: Kingswood.

White, Ellen G.
   1946   *Evangelism*. Washington, D.C.: Review and Herald.

Yoder, John Howard
   1994   *The Politics of Jesus: Vicit Agnus Noster*. 2d rev. ed. Grand Rapids: Eerdmans.

World Council of Churches
   1983   *Mission and Evangelism: An Ecumenical Affirmation: A Study Guide*. Geneva: World Council of Churches.

Index

ABFMS, 30-31

Abolitionist, 18-21, 35

Abraham, William J., 60, 62, 64, 133, 167, 169

Acts, 4, 11, 14-15, 38-39, 47, 60-62, 67, 70, 74, 78, 89-91, 93-96, 106-109, 115-116, 121-122, 135, 156, 160, 163-165, 170-171, 175

Adams, Roy, 138, 148-149, 168

Adventists, 15, 20, 136, 138, 154-155, 167-168, 170-173, 175, 183-184

Africa, 7, 127, 152

African-American, 20

Ageism, 147

America(n), 19-20, 24, 28-32, 34, 36-37, 42, 44, 135, 145, 147, 151-154, 158, 166-167, 171, 173-174

American Baptist Foreign Missionary Society, 30-31

Amillennialists, 27, 162

Anglican, 18

Antioch, 95

Arias, Mortimer, 63, 77, 80, 91, 94-95, 104, 141, 145, 168

Aristides, 17

Arthur, William, 22

Asia Minor, 91

Auburn Affirmation, 30

Baptist Missionary, 30-31

Baptists, 19, 30-31, 157

Barr, James, 61, 163, 168

Barrett, David, 59-61, 120, 163, 168

Barrett, Kate and Waller, 23

Beelzebul, 97

Benedictus of Zechariah, 100-101, 110

Berlin World Congress on Evangelism, 35

Betrayal Commission, 32

Birch, Bruce C., 49, 52, 168

Boff, Leonardo, 93, 139, 168

Bosch, David J., 51-52, 60, 62, 64-66, 68, 70, 74, 79-80, 90-91, 100, 103-104, 108, 110, 112, 114-115, 117, 120, 127, 134, 142, 151, 164-166, 168-169

Brueggemann, Walter, 51, 59, 63-64, 67, 81, 132, 137, 144-145, 169

Brunt, John, 109, 111, 167, 169

Business(persons), 18, 22, 91

Cambridge, 18
Caribbean, 15. *Also see* Jamaica
Cassidy, Richard J., 83, 164, 169
Castro, Emilio, 39, 41, 65, 80-81, 94, 108, 134, 151, 169
Chicago Declaration, 36
Christian Missionary Alliance, 23
Christmas, 67, 81-82
Church growth movement, 11, 40-41, 43-44, 127-129, 149, 157, 176
Civil rights movement, 35, 39, 129, 147
Civil War, 18, 20-23
Clapham Sect, 18
Conn, Harvie M., 130, 150, 155, 175
Conversion, 36, 40, 62-63, 65, 81, 89, 93, 116-119, 122, 134, 131, 136, 143, 146, 161-162, 165, 174
Conzelmann, Hans, 54, 169
Cooper, Anthony Ashley, 18
Costas, Orlando, 19, 71, 169
Cox, Kenneth O., 154, 169
Crittondon, Florence and Charles, 23

Darwinian evolution, 27
David, king, 54, 56, 96, 100-101
Demonic, demons, 55, 69, 77-78, 81, 94, 97, 104, 107-109, 112, 140
Dennis, James S., 24-26, 170
Dispensationalists, 28-29, 125-126
Dyrness, William, 68, 88-90, 95, 146, 170

Easter, 98
Eastern Europe, 27; mind, 95
Economics. *See* Social justice
Ecumenical, ecumenism, 15, 30, 117, 133, 172-173, 175-176; Affimation, 117, 175-176
Egypt, 56
El Salvador, 157
Ephesus, 90, 95
Escobar, Samuel, 35-36, 90-91, 170
Evangelical(s), 7, 11, 15, 18-46, 53, 61, 123-125, 129-153, 163, 171-172, 174-175
Europe, 24, 36, 42, 121

Finney, Charles, 19-21
Forgiveness, 27, 60, 101, 109-117, 122, 144, 147
Fundamentalist-Modernist, Fundamentalists, 13, 24, 27-35, 44-46, 48, 123-125, 147, 159, 170-172

Gabriel, angel, 56, 75, 81
Gaebelein, Frank, 36
Galilee, 55, 97
Gallagher, Sharon, 36
Gaventa, Beverly Roberts, 57, 63, 115, 170
Gentiles, 75-76, 79, 87, 101, 116
Gloria in Excelsis Deo, 67
Gnostic, 13-14, 134
Great Awakenings, 18-20, 22, 42, 162
"Great Reversal," 28. *See also* Reversal motif
Green, Michael, 48, 61, 63, 74, 110, 151, 170
Greenwalt, Glen, 48-51, 170

Hades, 84
Hadrian, 17
Healing, health, 18, 55, 62-64, 67, 69, 76-77, 81, 90, 94, 103-109,

112, 121, 128, 140-142, 163, 165.
See also Salvation, physical
Hellenist, hellenization, 61, 121
Henry, Carl F. H., 33-34, 36, 170
Henry, Paul, 36
Herod, king, 56, 78, 81
Himes, Joshua V., 20
Hoekendijk, J. C., 139, 170
Holy Ghost/Spirit, 14, 22, 27, 47, 53, 90, 93, 96, 98, 108, 120-122, 131, 160, 165, 175
Hope, 15, 30, 32, 40, 64-79, 82, 86-88, 91, 101, 112, 135, 138-142, 144, 146, 157, 160-161, 164
Hunsberger, George R., 156, 171

Idaho, 155
Inspiration of Scripture, of the Spirit, 15, 48-53, 58, 98, 122, 150, 166, 170
International Congress on World Evangelism, 37

Jamaica, 137, 152, 154, 183
James, book of, 10-11, 49, 91, 163, 166, 171-172, 184
Jeremias, Joachim, 164, 171
Jerusalem, 29, 86, 89, 96, 104, 114-115, 121-122
Jesus Movement, 100, 138
John, Gospel of, 38-39, 55, 104, 149, 163
John the Baptist, 14, 57, 61, 65, 72, 82, 84-85, 91, 101-103, 110-117, 119-124, 135, 156, 160, 163, 165
Jubilee, 70-71, 112
Judea, 56, 81, 96, 115
Justice. *See* Social justice
Justification (doctrine), 99

Kantian philosophy, 27

Keck, Leander E., 54, 171
Kingdom. *See* Reign of God; Rule of God
Krass, Alfred, 39, 46, 51, 62, 80, 99, 147, 153, 171

Ladd, George Eldon, 93, 171
Lausanne (Committee/Covenant/Statement), 37, 40-42, 129
Linden, Ingemar, 20, 171
Linder, Robert, 28-29, 34, 171
Luke, Gospel of, 4, 11, 14-15, 38-39, 47, 49, 54-58, 59-90, 92-125, 127-128, 131, 133, 135, 138, 140, 145-146, 149-150, 153, 156, 160, 165, 169, 171, 173, 175
Luke's great commission, 105, 113-116, 125

Magnificat, 65-67, 81-83, 100-101, 111
Marginal(ized people), 18, 55-57, 64-74, 79, 88, 91, 92, 100, 113, 122, 134-135, 139, 142, 147, 160-161
Mark, Gospel of, 38, 54-55, 66, 86, 102-103, 107, 113, 120, 162-163, 165
Marsden, George M., 28, 31, 171
Materialism, 36, 83, 145, 147, 149
Matthew, Gospel of, 15, 39, 49, 54-57, 61, 66, 68, 71, 75, 86-87, 102, 113, 120, 126, 130, 134, 163-166
Matthew's great commission, 14, 34, 47, 61, 68, 113, 115, 123, 125, 160, 163
Maynard-Reid, Pedrito U., 7-12, 69, 84-86, 164, 171-172, 183-184
McAuley, J. A., 23
McGavran, Donald A., 11, 40, 127-129, 172

Messiah, 55, 60, 60, 68, 75, 101, 107, 113, 117-118, 146-147, 161
Metanoia, 117-118, 146-147, 161
Methodists, 19, 21-22
Miles, Delos, 17-19, 130-131, 146, 158, 166, 172
Militarism, 36, 40
Millennium, millennialism, 21, 27-28, 34, 162, 169, 175
Millerites, 20
Missio Dei, 127, 135
Missionary conferences, 35, 39, 41
Modernists. *See* Fundamentalists
Monkey Trial, 29
Moody, Dwight L., 22
Motte, Mary, 139-140, 172
Mouw, Richard J., 40, 133, 172

Nazareth, 12, 55, 68, 71-72, 104, 106-108, 114, 120, 139-140
Newbigin, Lesslie, 131-133, 171-172
Niebuhr, H. Richard, 174
North America, 34-36, 42, 44, 92, 135, 147, 151-154, 157, 172. *See also* America
Northwest (of U.S.), 15, 137, 152, 155-156, 167, 174
Nunc Dimittis, 101

Oberlin, 19, 21
Oosterwal, Gottfried, 151, 172
Oregon, 155-156
Orthodox Catholic, 16

Palestine, Palestinian, 51, 74, 80-81, 96-97, 100, 104, 137, 142, 164, 172
Pannell, William, 23, 99, 103, 125, 167
Pattaya, Thailand, 41

Patterson, James Alan, 23, 28-32, 162, 172
Paul, apostle, 15, 47, 49, 60, 62, 74, 79, 91, 95, 99, 110, 116, 120-121, 123, 126, 153, 167
Paulien, Jon K., 153, 172
Pentecost (day), 78, 89-90, 121
Pentecostal, 22
Perrin, Norman, 43-54, 173
Peter, apostle, 74, 78, 88, 90-91, 106, 108, 115-116, 121, 124
Peters, George W., 125-126, 173
Pierson, Paul E., 173, 175
Pippert, Rebecca Manley, 135, 151-152, 173
Pixley, G. V., 27-98, 173
Politics, 16, 18, 21-22, 28-29, 31, 34-38, 40, 44, 50, 80-81, 90-91, 93-94, 96, 99-101, 109-111, 118, 121-122, 125, 133-134, 137, 141-143, 145-147, 150, 159, 166, 169, 172, 176. *See also* Salvation, political
Poor, the, 5, 19, 21, 37, 65-74, 79-90, 100, 118-119, 122, 134, 137, 139-142, 160-161, 163-165, 168, 171-172, 184
Portland, Oregon, 156
Posterski, Donald C., 89, 146, 153, 173, 165
Postmillennialists, 27-28, 162
Potter, Philip, 119, 135, 173
Premillennialists, 27-28, 34, 162
Presbyterians, 20, 24-27, 30
Primitive church, 15, 62, 74, 79, 89-90, 108, 116, 121-122
Princeton Theological Seminary, 24-27
Proclamation, 19, 32, 34, 36-37, 40, 42, 59-63, 68, 76, 91, 101-103, 106, 112-115, 124, 131-134,

138-139, 148, 156, 165-166, 171
Protestant, 15, 18-32, 49-50, 172

Qumran, 104, 164

Racism, 23, 35-37, 74, 129, 137, 147
Ramm, Bernard, 36
Rasi, Humberto M., 167, 170, 172-173
Rauschenbusch, Walter, 125, 166, 173
Rees, Paul, 36
Reign of God, kingdom of God/heaven, 12, 15, 24, 29, 37, 39, 42, 57, 60, 64-65, 71-100, 103, 105-109, 118-122, 124, 126, 131-157, 160-164, 168-169, 171, 173, 175. *See also* Rule of God.
entrance into, 79, 81-82, 84-88, 90, 103-104, 109, 118-119, 137-138, 140-141, 147
inauguration of, 65, 96, 108, 112
initiation and invitation into, 16, 38, 45, 64, 71, 91, 98, 120-122, 124, 132, 134-135, 137, 152, 158, 166
manifestations of, 72, 108
opposition to, 15, 35, 81-82, 109, 124, 160-161
Repent, repentance, 36-37, 47, 57, 60, 65, 76, 80, 82, 88, 93, 109-122, 143-147, 161
Resurrection, 17, 37, 60-61, 72, 77-78, 98, 147
Reversal motif, 66-67, 83, 100, 102-103, 111
Rice, George, 54, 102, 105, 107, 113, 163, 165, 173
Rich, the, 65-66, 70, 72, 81, 83-86,

88-90, 91, 100, 146, 164, 171
Rich ruler, 85, 88-89, 103, 118
Ro, Bong Rin, 19, 22, 24, 27, 173
Rockefeller, John D. Jr., 31
Roman Catholic, 15, 175
Roxburgh, Alan J., 148, 151, 157-158, 174
Rule of God, 24, 57, 94-95, 98, 162, 165. *See also* Reign of God

Sabbath, 77, 107-108
Salvation, 18-21, 23, 29-30, 38-40, 45, 47, 50, 54, 63, 68, 70, 72-74, 89-90, 93, 98-110, 113, 119, 122, 124, 126-127, 130, 133-134, 138, 140, 142, 146, 149, 157, 161, 166
eternal, 40, 43, 85-86, 88, 94, 103, 126, 133, 166
experience of, 21-22, 89, 98, 127, 133, 138-142, 150, 165
future, 15, 24, 64, 72-73, 95-98, 108, 124, 126-127, 138, 161, 166
personal, 11, 13-15, 18-32, 37-41, 44-45, 47, 50-51, 63, 65, 68, 73, 94, 98-99, 104, 106, 109, 118-119, 122, 134, 127-129, 132, 134-135, 137-144, 148-151, 156, 159-160, 165-167
physical, 25, 69-70, 72, 81, 94, 99-100, 104, 106-107, 112-113, 121-122, 134, 140-141, 148. *See also* Healing, health
political, 15, 21-22, 28-29, 31, 34-35, 37-38, 40, 44, 50, 80-81, 90-91, 93-101, 109-111, 118, 121-122, 125, 133-134, 137, 141-150, 169, 166, 172. *See also* Politics
social, 100-103, 110, 113. *See also* Social justice
wholistic, 62, 79, 94, 105, 109-113, 123-125, 128, 133, 135-137,

152, 156-158, 160-161, 166-167
Samaritans, 79, 95-96, 100, 105-
106, 115
Satan, 32, 81, 106-109, 116, 162
Saul. *See* Paul
Schniewind, Julius, 118, 165, 174
Scofield, Cyrus; Scofield Bible, 28
Schwantes, Carlos, 155, 174
Scopes, 29
Scriven, Charles, 136, 174
Seattle, 137, 152, 154-155, 157
Second advent/coming, 13, 20, 138
Second Great Awakening, 19, 162
Senior, Donald, 47, 94, 98, 104, 106, 140, 174
Sermon on a Level Place (Luke 6:17-49), 55, 65, 86
Sermon on the Mount (Matt. 5–7), 55, 68, 71, 86
Seventh-day Adventists. *See* Adventists
Seventy, the, 105, 107, 122, 164
Sexism, 36, 147
Shaftesbury, (seventh) Lord, 18
Sider, Ronald J., 36-37, 44, 62, 74-75, 77-78, 99-100, 129-130, 164, 174
Simpson, A. B., 23
Sine, Tom, 44, 71, 74, 98-99, 126, 137, 144, 146, 156-157, 166, 168, 170, 174-175
Slavery, 18-21, 35, 69, 71, 75, 78-79, 90, 109, 165
Smith, Linda, 35, 39-40, 174
Smith, Timothy, 21-23, 27, 29, 34, 174
Social Gospel, 23, 28, 30, 33, 35, 42, 125, 166, 173
Social justice/action, socioeconomic, 10-45, 63, 69-71, 90, 93,

96, 100, 103, 112, 119, 126, 130-131, 134, 138-139, 142-143, 145-147, 149, 157, 161, 163
Sociological force, 24-27, 63
Stott, John, 40, 165, 174
Stransky, Thomas F., 142, 146-147, 175
Strayer, Brian E., 20, 175
Stromberg, Jean, 117, 175
Switzerland. *See* Lausanne

Tannehill, Robert C., 66-69, 71-72, 74, 86, 89, 100-101, 104, 106-107, 111, 114-116, 163-164, 175
Tienou, Titi, 39, 111, 175
Two-thirds world, 34, 41, 45, 92, 137, 154

Valentine, Foy, 36
Van Engen, Charles, 7-9, 11, 33-34, 40-41, 45, 52, 62-63, 135-136, 141, 152, 163, 165, 169, 175
Verkuyl, J., 54, 94, 133, 162, 175

Wagner, C. Peter, 11, 43, 149, 175
Wallis, Jim, 36, 40, 44, 63, 88, 99, 118, 143, 146-147, 176
Washington, state of, 12, 155, 184
Watson, David Lowes, 133, 135, 143-144, 151, 166, 176
Wesleyan, 21, 23, 176
White, Ellen G., 155, 176
Wilberforce, William, 18, 35
World Conference, 41
World Council of Churches. *See* Ecumenical
World Evangelical Fellowship, 41
Yoder, John Howard, 176
YMCA, 22
Zacchaeus, 65, 73-74, 88-89, 105, 120-121, 146

The Author

Pedrito Uriah Maynard-Reid was born on July 10, 1947, in Kingston, Jamaica, to Edith Maynard-Reid and Harry Reid. After primary and secondary schooling in Kingston, he graduated from Kingsway High School, then earned a B.Th. from West Indies College, Mandeville, Jamaica, in 1970. At Andrews University, Berrien Springs, Michigan, he earned an M.A. in church history in 1973, an M.Div. in 1975, and a Th.D. in New Testament exegesis and theology in 1981.

Maynard-Reid was baptized at the age of ten in the Seventh-Day Adventist Church, and was ordained to its ministry on November 28, 1978. He has served in Jamaica as senior pastor of the West Indies College Church. He held the rank of professor in the departments of religion and theology both at West Indies College, Jamaica, and Antillian College, Puerto Rico. In both places he also chaired the departments.

On August 23, 1970, he married Violet Thompson of Mandeville. They have two children, Pedrito II and Natascha. The Maynard-Reids are members of Walla Walla College Church, where Pedrito is an associate head elder. Both are on the faculty of Walla Walla College in College

Place, Washington State, USA. Violet is the reference librarian, and Pedrito is professor of biblical studies and missiology. Since 1970 he has taught ministerial students in Jamaica, Puerto Rico, Mexico, and the states of Michigan and Washington.

Pedrito Maynard-Reid has published articles and a book, *Poverty and Wealth in James* (Orbis, 1987). On joining the faculty of Walla Walla's School of Theology in 1990, he began studying for the degree of Th.M. in missiology at Fuller Theological Seminary, continuing his studies through subsequent summers. He continues to hold seminars on the interrelatedness of faith and action, evangelism and social concern.